John George Wood

Half Hours with a Naturalist

Rambles Near the Shore

John George Wood

Half Hours with a Naturalist
Rambles Near the Shore

ISBN/EAN: 9783337025540

Printed in Europe, USA, Canada, Australia, Japan

Cover: Foto ©Andreas Hilbeck / pixelio.de

More available books at **www.hansebooks.com**

THE HALF HOUR LIBRARY
OF TRAVEL, NATURE, AND SCIENCE
FOR YOUNG READERS

HALF HOURS WITH A NATURALIST

𝔑ambles near the 𝔖hore

BY THE REV. J. G. WOOD, M.A.
AUTHOR OF "HALF HOURS IN FIELD AND FOREST"
"HOMES WITHOUT HANDS," ETC.

WITH NUMEROUS ILLUSTRATIONS

LONDON
CHARLES BURNET & CO.
9, BUCKINGHAM STREET, STRAND.
1889

LONDON:
PRINTED BY J. S. VIRTUE AND CO., LIMITED,
CITY ROAD.

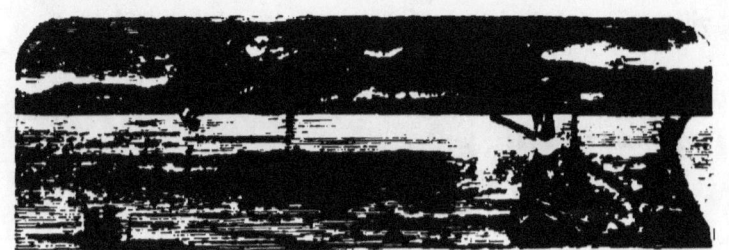

CONTENTS.

FAIRY LAND AMONG THE SPONGES.

CHAP.		PAGE
I.	WONDERS OF SPONGE STRUCTURE	3
II.	THE EUPLECTELLA, OR VENUS'S SEA-BASKET	12
III.	THE ROSSELLA VELATA	20

HOMES UNDER THE SEA.

		PAGE
I.	CUTTLEFISHES, THE OCTOPUS, &C.	29
II.	THE COMMON SEPIA	37
III.	SEA STARS OR STARFISHES	44
IV.	WHAT ARE THE STARFISHES?	55
V.	SEA URCHINS	63
VI.	,, MATERIAL AND DEVELOPMENT	74

SOME WONDERS OF THE SEA.

CHAP.		PAGE
I.	JELLY FISHES	85
II.	,, POISONOUS STING	93
III.	,, VARIETY AND BEAUTY	104
IV.	CORALS	122
V.	,, FORM AND ACHIEVEMENTS	137

THE MOST GIFTED INSECT RACE.

I.	ANT LIFE	149
II.	THEIR MODE OF FIGHTING	162
III.	PLUNDER AND SLAVE-CATCHING	167
IV.	FOOD AND FORAGING EXPEDITIONS	173
V.	THEIR ARCHITECTURE	178

THE MARVEL OF INSECT LIFE.

I.	SOLITARY BEES: THEIR HABITS AND WORK	187
II.	HUMBLE BEES: THEIR HOUSEKEEPING	197
III.	HIVE BEES: THEIR DISCIPLINE AND HARMONY	204
IV.	HONEY BEES: THE PRINCIPLE OF ORDER	211
V.	THE MYSTERY OF HONEY AND WAX	217
VI.	LET NOTHING BE LOST	223
VII.	BEES SPEAK A LANGUAGE	229

ABOUT SPIDERS AND THEIR WEBS.

I.	LAND SPIDERS	235
II.	THE VENOM-BEARERS—THE BIRD SPIDER	248
III.	TRAP-DOOR SPIDERS	253
IV.	WATER SPIDERS	258

SOME NOXIOUS INSECTS

CHAP.		PAGE
I	INJURIOUS TO MAN	267
II.	WOOL AND WOOD DESTROYERS	276
III.	OUR BENEFACTORS	285

DRAGON-FLIES.

I.	THEIR LIFE HISTORY	295
II.	THEIR APPALLING VORACITY	302

THE HORSE AND HIS STRUCTURE.

I.	THE LEFT OR NEAR FOREFOOT	311
II.	THE HOOF, SOLE, ETC.	317
III.	THE SHOE AND THE FROG	323
IV.	THE HEAD AND NECK	331

LIST OF ILLUSTRATIONS.

	PAGE
HOMES UNDER THE SEA . . . . *Frontispiece*	
GLASS-ROPE SPONGE	6
EUPLECTELLA ASPERGILLUM, OR VENUS'S SEA-BASKET . .	9
SPICULES OF GLASS-SPONGES, UNDER THE MICROSCOPE .	15
EUPLECTELLA CUCUMER	17
ROSSELLA VELATA	23
THE OCTOPUS	32
EXTREMITY OF ARM	35
THE COMMON SEPIA	38
CUTTLE BONE	39
EGGS OF SEPIA	41
FIVE-FINGERED STARFISH	46
UNDER-SURFACE OF STARFISH	48
STARFISH REPRODUCING MISSING PORTIONS . . .	51
ENCRINITES, OR LILY-STONES	55
COMATULA, OR FEATHER STAR	57
GORGONOCEPHALUS, OR GORGON'S HEAD . . .	59
BRITTLE STARS, OR SNAKE-TAIL	61

LIST OF ILLUSTRATIONS.

	PAGE
SEA URCHIN.	64
MAMILLATED URCHIN STRIPPED OF ITS SPINES	66
MAMILLATED URCHIN.	67
SHELL OF SEA URCHIN	69
SECTION OF SEA URCHIN	71
SYNAPTA	77, 79
UMBRELLA JELLY FISH	87, 88
RHIZOSTOMA, OR ROOT-MOUTHED.	95
RHIZOSTOMA.	99
PLAYA DIPHYES	112
THE PHYSOPHORES	115
SOME WONDERS OF THE SEA	123
MUSHROOM MADREPORE	127
PLANTAIN MADREPORE.	131
GOBLET CARYOPHYLLE.	135
A SECTION OF CORAL	139
CORAL POLYPES	140
SEA FAN	141
ORGAN-PIPE CORAL	143, 144
ANTS	152
ANTS DRAGGING BEETLE	156
ANTS AND THEIR TINY GRUBS	157
OSMIA BURROWS	190
MEGACHILE BURROW	190
ROSE-CUTTER BEES AND NEST	192
XYLOCOPA, OR CARPENTER BEE	194
DRONE. QUEEN. WORKER.	198
CARDER BEES AT WORK	199
HUMBLE BEES AND CELLS	201
CARDER BEES. EXTERIOR OF NEST	202
CARDER BEES. INTERIOR OF NEST	203
SECTION OF COMB.	205
HIVE BEE. EDGE OF COMB WITH ROYAL CELL.	206
SWARM.	208

LIST OF ILLUSTRATIONS.

	PAGE
HONEY BEES AT WORK	213
WAITING FOR THE BEES SWARMING	219
PLACING THE SWARM IN THEIR NEW HIVE	225
THE GARDEN SPIDER	236
SPIDER'S WEB ON WILD MUSTARD	239
SPIDER'S WEB IN OATS	243
MONEY-SPINNERS	246
THE BIRD SPIDER	250
TRAP-DOOR SPIDER	255
WATER SPIDERS	259
LOCUST	269
MIGRATORY LOCUST	270
PALM, OR GRU-GRU, WEEVIL	271
NESTS OF WHITE ANT OR TERMITES	272
THE CLOTHES MOTH	277
SCOLYTUS DESTRUCTOR TUNNELS	279
MUSK BEETLE	280
GOAT-MOTH CATERPILLAR	281
GREAT TERMITE	282
BUTTERFLIES	286
SILKWORMS	287
HONEY ANT	290
DRAGON-FLY: ITS THREE STAGES	297
DRAGON-FLY LARVA TAKING ITS PREY	299
DRAGON-FLY BEING RELEASED	304
THE DRAGON-FLY	306
BONES OF PASTERN	312
SECTION OF PASTERN	313
UNDER SURFACE, UNTOUCHED HOOF	318
HORSE-HOOF, IMPROVED BY THE FARRIER	319
FRONT OF HOOF: TRANSVERSE SECTION	320
"CHARLIER" SHOE, MODIFIED BY FLEMING	326
LIGAMENTS AND VERTEBRÆ OF THE HORSE'S HEAD	333
THE "GAG" BEARING-REIN	335

FAIRY LAND AMONG THE SPONGES.

B

FAIRY LAND AMONG THE SPONGES.

CHAPTER I.

WONDERS OF SPONGE STRUCTURE.

NATURE is always intolerant of human presumption. Man collects some facts, generalises upon them, establishes theories delightfully satisfactory to their originator, and then settles down in proud consciousness of his own wisdom. But he is not long allowed to rest. Out of her measureless treasure-houses Nature produces some fact equally unexpected and incontrovertible, and the old-established theories melt away like snow-wreaths before the spring-tide sun.

Not the least among the advantages of physical science is, that those who really study it for its own sake, learn day by day how little they know, and so far from being vain of their knowledge, are humiliated by their ignorance. Of all created beings the highest archangel must be the most humble, because he knows the most.

We do not even know the distinctive marks which separate animal from vegetable life. Locomotion was for many years accepted as the proof of animal life, and the volvoces which roll ceaselessly through the water, and the diatoms which dart about as swiftly as the whirling beetles, and avoid collision with equal dexterity, were ranked among the animals.

Now, however, all these minute beings have been proved to belong to the simplest forms of vegetable life, and the Locomotive Theory had to be abandoned.

Among the beings which occupy the border-land between the animal and vegetable kingdoms, the SPONGES have of late years started into prominence. Relegated at first to the vegetable, but now conclusively proved to belong to the animal kingdom, the sponges are full of interest to the student of zoology.

With the sponge of commerce we are all familiar enough, and it is scarcely necessary to state that it consists of the horny skeleton alone, the whole of the organic matter having been removed. This organic matter is apparently nothing but a mere wash or film of gelatinous substance covering every filament of the skeleton; but when carefully examined it presents a most remarkable mixture of simplicity and complication.

Without entering into the purely scientific details of sponge-structure, I will endeavour to lay open some of the wonders which are hidden in one of the lowest forms of animal life.

In order to appreciate the life of a sponge, it will be necessary to examine a living specimen. To procure a living marine sponge is not very easy; but the fresh-water sponges are common enough, and will answer our purpose just as well. They may be procured in almost any slow-flowing river, and are adherent to twigs and similar objects that have remained in the water for some length of time.

At Oxford I used to find them in the Cherwell and Isis, mostly attached to willow twigs that drooped into the water. The still water near a lock is a favourite spot for them, and in sheets of fresh water they are wonderfully numerous. The great Swindon reservoir is so full of them that any amount may be procured in an hour or so.

Take one of these sponges, the smaller the better, and place it in a glass vessel. A common watch-glass will answer the purpose admirably. Presently, distinct currents will be perceptible in the water, especially if a little carmine or indigo be dissolved in it. Prussian blue is poisonous, but the "blue" used by the laundress is safe enough. Carmine, however, is, in my opinion, better than any blue tint, as it is prettier in general effect, and the particles are so transparent that they do not become opaque when collected together.

When the currents are fairly established, the magnifying glass will exhibit a wonderful phase of animal life.

The whole of the surface of the sponge is covered with little prominences, having at the tip of each a tolerably large aperture. Through this hole the coloured water pours outwards, causing the currents which have made themselves visible.

But how did these coloured particles, which rush out with such force, get into the sponge at all? A more powerful lens will solve the problem. The whole of the surface is studded with innumerable little holes, piercing through the gelatinous membrane and admitting the water into the interior of the sponge. A section of the sponge will show that these little holes lead into canals which travel in every direction through the substance of the sponge, and finally lead to the larger apertures through which the water is ejected.

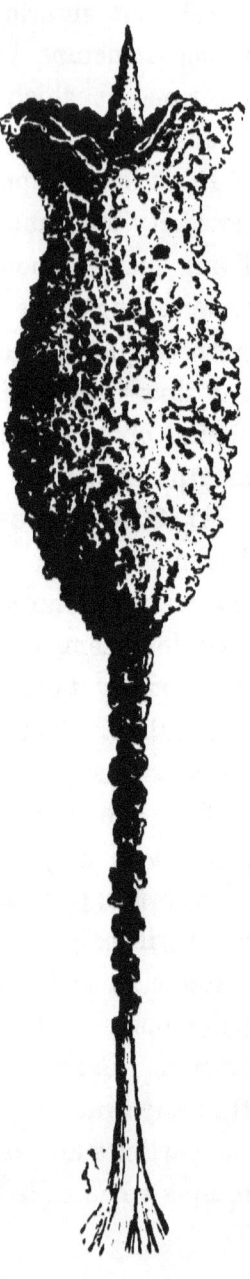

Fig. 1.—GLASS-ROPE SPONGE (*Hyalonema Lausitanicum*). Half real size.

Every now and then the current stops and all the tiny orifices are closed, without even a mark to show where they had been. Presently it begins again, and then it will be seen that the former orifices are not reopened, but that fresh apertures are developed as they are wanted.

Now we may ask ourselves how these larger apertures are kept open, and to answer the question we must call chemistry to our aid. In some sponges we can use the blow-pipe, but as a general rule some strong acid or caustic alkali will destroy the whole of the animal matter. If the residuum be examined with the microscope, a vast number of glassy spicules will be seen, varying in shape, size, and colour with the kind of sponge.

Some of them look exactly as if they were made of pink and white sugar-candy, and all children to whom I have shown them have expressed regret at their inability to eat such tempting objects. Those of the ordinary sponge have the most striking resemblance to the "crow's-feet," or "caltrops," which were once used to impede the progress of cavalry. It is said that these spiculæ vary according to the substance on which the sponge is fixed, as well as in the species; but I have had no opportunity of testing this theory, and content myself with mentioning it.

The structure of the ordinary marine and fresh-water sponges having been carefully studied, zoologists set about the very necessary task of classifying them. Considering the nature of the subject, this was no easy task and almost as many systems were promulgated as there were zoologists to write about them. Meanwhile Nature had her rebuff ready to produce, and before it all the systems fell to pieces.

Rather more than forty years ago, Von Siebold brought from Japan, among other curiosities, some odd-looking objects provisionally called Glass-ropes. One of them is shown at Fig. 1, and is drawn about half its natural dimensions. What these odd things were, no one could say, and no one had seen anything like them. A bundle of long, rather brittle, translucent threads, was surrounded by a membrane, and at one end was an object which was evidently a sponge, the other end being attached to a small mass of coral.

These singular objects were submitted to many scientific men, and among others to Ehrenberg, the celebrated microscopist. After careful examination he pronounced that it was nothing but a zoological practical joke perpetrated by some ingenious Japanese.

He had certainly good reasons for mistrusting anything strange that came from Japan. The patient industry which enables a Japanese to be so "thorough" in his work, that in a metal bow not half an inch in length, every strand of the bowstring is separately twisted, and every joint in a tiny golden lobster's antennæ separately engraved, combined with a singularly quaint and delicate sense of humour, guide him not only in the legitimate province of Art, but in the playful ingenuities of sham monsters.

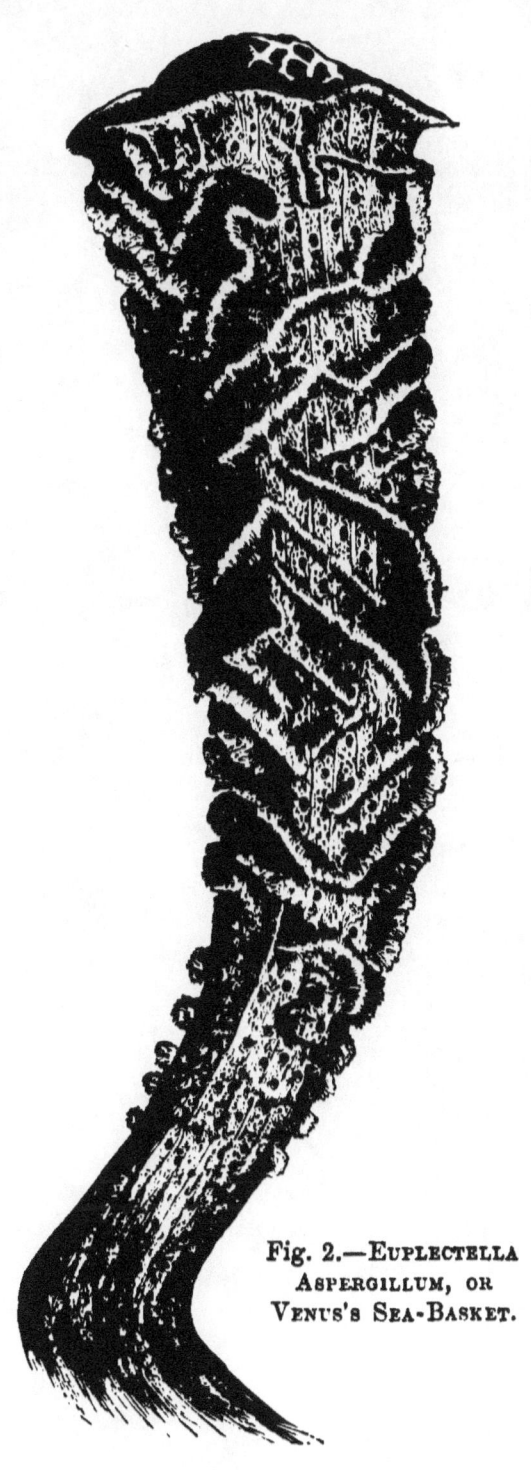

Fig. 2.—Euplectella Aspergillum, or Venus's Sea-Basket.

So, when such an extraordinary combination was found as a bundle of long glassy threads, pressed together with a membranous wrapper, and stuck into a sponge at one end and a lump of coral at the other, there was good justification for considering it as a mere piece of Japanese ingenuity. The constituent parts were evidently what they appeared to be. The sponge was certainly a sponge; no one could doubt the genuineness of the coral; the investing membrane was of an animal nature, and the wisp of long threads was certainly glass, its siliceous nature being ascertained by chemistry. A definite name was then given to it, *Hyalonema, i.e.* Glass-rope, and it was admitted to be a natural production.

By degrees additional specimens were discovered, but without the coral, as shown in Fig. 1. The coral was then seen to be a mere addition by way of improving the look of the specimen; but the glass threads still remained a mystery.

All this time the savants were battling about the true origin of the Hyalonema, some saying that the glass-wisp, envelope, and sponge were formed from coral; others that the glass-rope was formed by the sponge, and that the envelope was a "commensal polyp." Commensal, I may here explain, may be translated by the word "messmate," and in zoology it signifies a parasite which feeds with, but not upon, the being to which it is attached. This was a very close approximation to the truth, the envelope being, in truth, a mass of commensal polyps, which, when dried, shrivelled up into the thin, leathery membrane which had for so long been a mystery.

FAIRY LAND AMONG THE SPONGES.

CHAPTER II.

THE EUPLECTELLA, OR VENUS'S SEA-BASKET.

ANOTHER great surprise was at hand, when the wonderful *Euplectella*, or Venus's Sea-Basket, was discovered. Whatever might have been the case with the Hyalonema, the Euplectella could not be of human construction. (See page 9.)

The ingenious Japanese could make a mermaid from papier-mâché moulded over a carefully constructed skeleton. He could work fish-skin into its substance while wet, prick hairs into it with patient assiduity, and with equal foresight intermingle the hairs with tiny fish-scales. He could fill the half-opened mouth with strange teeth, but no human fingers could weave the glassy meshes of the Euplectella, any more than they could frame the starry crystals of the snow-flake.

The membranous envelope was not found in the Euplectella; a tuft of glassy threads like newly carded wool sprang from the base, and the glass-threads of the body, instead of being loosely twisted together in rope fashion, were woven into an exquisitely shaped vase, almost exactly representing the cornucopia of the ancients, and closed with a perforated lid very much like the rose of a watering-pot.

As to the pattern, a verbal description is almost useless, and the representation at Fig. 2 can give but a faint idea of its general aspect. It looks as if it were made of the finest imaginable lace, each thread being of pure white glass, and not so thick as a human hair. As in basket-work, stronger threads form the framework, and upon them the intricate, though beautifully regular, pattern of the meshes is woven.

Frills of this delicate lace are laid with artistic carelessness around the upper part of the basket, and the effect of the pure white threads, with the opalescent hues that flit over them with every change of light, baffles all description. The dreams of fairy land pale before the realities of ocean-life, and the mind of man could no more have conceived, than his fingers could have executed, the work which is done by a film of animated jelly in the darkness of the sea-depth.

There was just a possibility that the glass-rope was the work of human hands, but no one thought for a moment that the Euplectella could have been designed, much less formed, by man. The most accomplished naturalists were the most astonished when the Euplectella was first brought to the light of day, and could only sit and gaze in silence and bewildered admiration.

As is always the case with the works of the Creator, the microscope, one of His latest and best gifts to man, reveals more and greater wonders than can be visible to the unassisted eye.

It has already been mentioned that the skeleton of the sponges is formed of many-pointed and differently shaped spicules. But when the spicules of the Euplectella were placed under the microscope they were found to excel in beauty and variety those of the ordinary sponges as much as the sea-baskets excel in external appearance the sponges of commerce.

A few of the spicules most generally found in the various glass-sponges are given in the accompanying illustration (Fig. 3). Formed apparently of the purest glass, with milky opalescent tints melting imperceptibly into each other, with their graceful curves and outlines drawn with a firm decision that baffles the best artist's pencil, they are of such minute dimensions that the six-rayed spicule at A *e* is only one thirteen-hundredth of an inch in diameter. Were it further magnified, fresh beauties would be discovered at every increase of magnifying power.

Beginning with A, which represents some spicules of an Euplectella, *a* is an " anchoring filament ; " *b b b b* are spicules from the "sarcode," *i.e.*, the animated jelly above mentioned; *c d* are two of the six-rayed spicules in course of formation; and *e* represents the completed spicule.

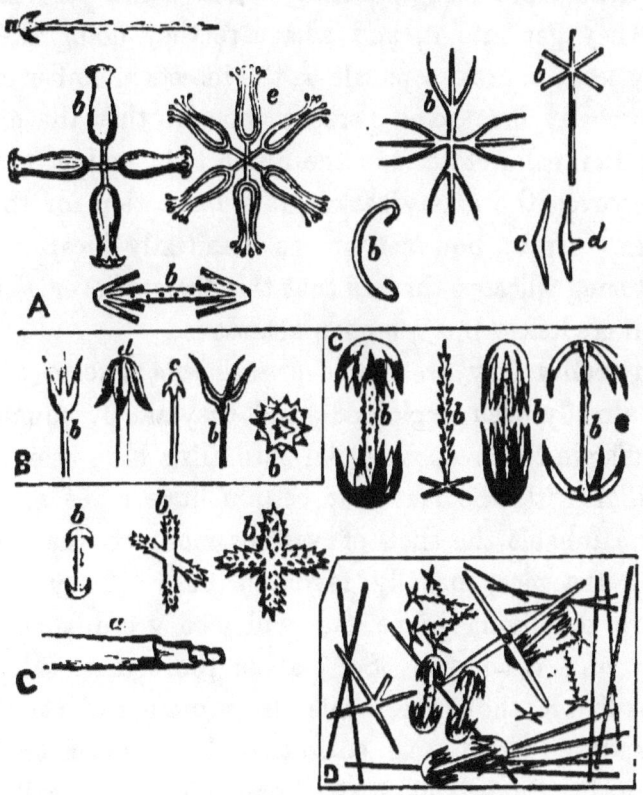

Fig. 3.—SPICULES OF GLASS-SPONGES, AS THEY APPEAR UNDER THE MICROSCOPE.

At B are shown the spicule-forms found in Tethya; C shows spicules of the glass-rope (*Hyalonema*), and D shows a group of the spicules as they appear in their ordinary positions.

The reader may remember that the mouth of the vase is closed with a perforated lid woven of the same glassy substance as its walls; yet this vase is mostly inhabited, two little crabs being generally found within it. How did they get into it, and what are they doing there? They seem as great a puzzle as the insects in amber used to be. At first some persons thought that the crabs were the real architects of the Euplectella, and that they had woven the glassy basket as a habitation for themselves. Crabs, however, are so manifestly incapable of producing siliceous threads that this theory never gained much credence, and was soon abandoned.

In reality they are simple commensals, a term which has already been explained; and they are by no means singular in this respect. All naturalists have been long familiar with the fact that certain little crabs (*Pinnotheres*) inhabit the shell of various molluscs, the pinna being the most usually favoured host. They never injure the living pinna, but will feed greedily on the body of a dead one. So, just as the commensal pea-crabs live in the pinna, while the substance of the shell is deposited round them, so do these little messmates live within the Euplectella basket, remaining there while its glassy meshes are being woven around them. Why either of these crustacea should choose such remarkable habitations no one knows.

Of these Euplectella there are many species. To all appearance the animated jelly is exactly the same throughout all the tribe, but each has its own form of

Fig. 4.—EUPLECTELLA CUCUMER. Half real size.

spicule, and its own mode of weaving its glass basket. A well-defined species is here shown. As it resembles a gourd rather than a horn in shape, it has received the scientific name of *Euplectella cucumer* (Fig. 4).

Different as it may be in outline, it still possesses the perforated lid, the elaborate mesh-work of the body, and the wisp of filmy glass threads at the bottom.

In this species, perhaps more than any other, we cannot but be struck with an uneasy sensation that cane-seated chairs must in some mysterious way have derived their origin from the Euplectella. Cane-seated chairs were used by the Egyptians three thousand years ago, their pattern being exactly like that of the chair on which I am now sitting. The Euplectella was, I believe, unknown before 1840, and yet the resemblance between the pattern of the sponge and that of the chair is so startling, that the most unobservant cannot fail to notice it.

FAIRY LAND AMONG THE SPONGES.

CHAPTER III.

THE ROSSELLA VELATA.

HAVING somewhat of the same general shape as the species which has just been described, the *Rossella velata* (Fig. 5) is easily distinguishable by the mode in which the glassy fibres are woven together. Instead of leaving the regular "interstices between the intersections," as network does, the fibres are laid together so as to form a series of protuberances very much resembling those of the pineapple, and almost exactly like those of the less-known durian of Malacca.

The mode in which they are placed is not easy to describe, but may be understood by a reference to the illustration, and can be imitated in a very simple manner.

Take a number of the longest and finest entomological pins, draw a circle of about one-third of an inch in diameter on a piece of soft leather, and thrust the pins closely together up to their heads through the circular line. Pass an elastic band round them, at about half an inch from the leather, and they will form a double cone, the pins of the lower cone being closely set together, and those of the upper cone diverging at their points. Suppose that the leather were completely covered with similar circles, all set full of pins, and then stretched over a swan's egg, the appearance would almost precisely resemble that of the Rossella.

The points of the radiating pins would interlace with each other, so as to give a sort of uncertain filmy outline. In the Rossella, the glass threads are so fine and so translucent that their intermingling ends seem to form a sort of cloudy veil over the drab surface, thus earning for the sponge the appropriate name of *velata*, or "veiled."

Anchored in mud by their glittering cables, these wonderful beings have come from the ocean depths as if to show the extent of man's ignorance. Not long ago, no theory was held to be more firmly established than that of the absence of life in the depths of the sea. In an arctic temperature, in black darkness, under the terrific pressure of superincumbent water, plus that of the atmosphere above it, vegetation, and consequently animal life, was held to be impossible. All life was said to disappear beyond a certain depth from the surface;

six hundred fathoms, or about two-thirds of a mile, being given as the extreme limit of life, whether vegetable or animal. All the vast expanse below it was assumed to be a still, silent, dead desolation.

But when the great deep-sea sounding expeditions were undertaken, and specimens of the sea-bed were raised from a depth of more than five miles, it was found that there was no profundity to which the plummet could penetrate that did not produce examples of animal life, some of them so delicate and so elaborately constructed, that no one who saw them for the first time could imagine that they could have sustained the tremendous weight above them. Marvellous beauty of form was found at depths so great that until late years men could not reach the ocean bed with the plummet. Even now, when deep-sea sounding is studied as an art, so great is the friction of the water upon the wire rope, that when the weights have once reached the bottom of the sea, they cannot be drawn up again, but must be detached from the scrapers and left among the submarine life which they have been the means of discovering.

Until a few years ago, the eye of man never saw these beautiful forms, and up to the present time we have only seen some of those which occupied a few square inches of the sea bed. So with the glass-sponges. Who would not have thought that they were created to gladden the eye of man with their indescribable beauty? Had a stranger to them been asked in what seas they had been found, he would naturally have turned his

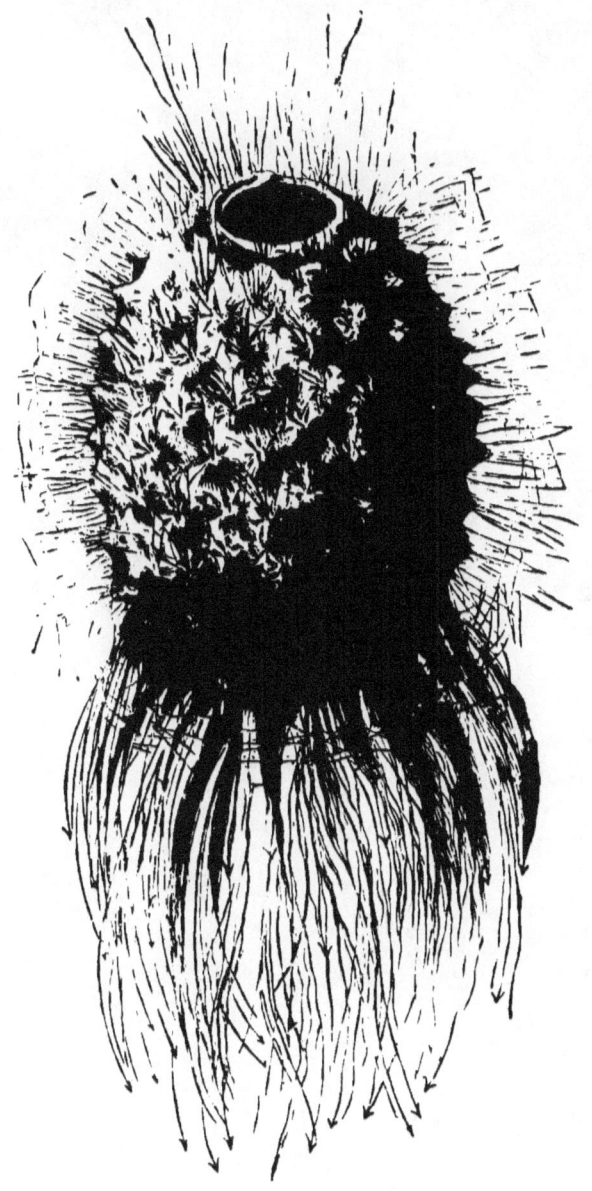

Fig. 5.—ROSSELLA VELATA. Half natural size.

mind to the shallow coral-reefs of the Pacific, where the water is warm, pure, and translucent, and where the hot sunbeams evoke the most brilliant hues in the fishes that dart through the water, as well as in the flowers that blossom on the shore.

Such is the locality in which man would have placed them. But He who made them knows best where to put them, and He knows that their right place is on mud, out of sight of man, at enormous depths, in impenetrable darkness and freezing cold. It seems as if we had been allowed to see these exquisite forms of hidden life, in order to show us that these hitherto unexplored depths teem with living beauty, and that in proportion as the sea gives up its treasures, we shall discover new developments of life as unexpected and, if possible, more beautiful than the glass-sponges which have added so much to our knowledge, and shown so plainly how much we have still to learn.

HOMES UNDER THE SEA.

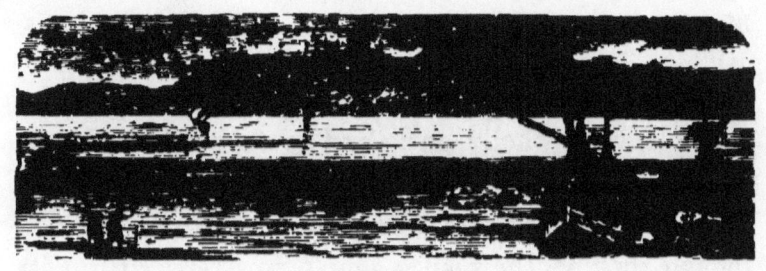

HOMES UNDER THE SEA.

CHAPTER 1.

CUTTLEFISHES, THE OCTOPUS, ETC.

SUPPOSE that we are watching a snail or a slug crawling up a pane of glass, we might readily imagine that it is as helpless a creature as can be found in the world.

It has no weapons of any kind. It cannot even resist when attacked, and much less can it assume the offensive. Its flesh is soft and yielding, and the muscular power is exceedingly feeble.

It is the prey of various creatures. The thrush and blackbird consume vast numbers of snails in the winter, and the hedgehog, when it breaks for awhile its hibernating slumbers, refreshes itself with the snails that, like itself, have been in hiding during the cold weather.

Several insects feed on the snail. The glow-worm, for example, lives wholly on it, and so does a little beetle which has no recognised popular name, but which is known to entomologists under the title of *Drilus*. Small though they be, the snail is simply powerless against its puny assailants, and submits quietly to be eaten alive.

Now, supposing that we were told that this soft-bodied creature could, by a few modifications of structure, be transformed into a fierce, voracious, active marauder of the seas, that the tender pliability of its structure would be one of its deadliest weapons, that the soft, yielding foot which slides gently over the glass, could become an instrument of prehension more to be dreaded than the talons of the tiger or the jaws of the boa, that it could be a more terrible foe than the shark itself, that it could shoot through the water with the speed of a rocket and on the same principle, and that it could project itself through the air completely over the hull of a large ship, we might be disposed to think that our informant was using the language of romance.

Yet, all these extraordinary conditions are fulfilled in the marine molluscs which are popularly, but wrongly, named Cuttle-fishes.

To begin, let us suppose that the foot of our slug is very much flattened and extended around the head. The creature does possess the power of extending and flattening the foot as it crawls, and we only have to imagine that, as it surrounds the head, to see that in that case the creature must crawl upon its head. This, indeed, is the origin of the scientific word Cephalopoda, or head-footed, to which all these creatures belong.

Next, we will suppose that this flat, circular foot is slit into a number of pointed, ribbon-like divisions, so that they radiate in starlike fashion from the head. Each of these rays would retain its power of expansion and contraction, and could act independently of the others. These rays, then, would constitute the arms, as they are called, of the Cuttle.

It is evident that if they could be made adhesive by some process, they could draw any object to which they clung towards the centre from which they radiate. And, if the mouth were to open upon that central point, it is also evident that the contraction of the rays would draw the object to the mouth.

It is also clear that the structure by which the rays are made adhesive, must be of such a nature that the hold can be loosened at will, as otherwise it would be obliged to swallow its arm as well as its food.

Both these conditions are fulfilled in the arms of the Cuttle.

The integuments of the under surface are modified into a double row of circular cups, the bottom of each cup being so made that it can be pushed into the hollow of the cup, or withdrawn at will, after the manner of a piston. Each of these cups acts as a sucker, as the reader will easily understand.

In its ordinary condition, the piston, as we may call it, nearly fills the cavity of the cup. When the creature wishes to seize upon any object, it presses the rim of the cup firmly against its surface, and withdraws the piston. A vacuum is therefore formed, and the pressure of the atmosphere, combined with that of the water, causes the cup to adhere strongly to the object. This power is increased according to the number and size of the cups, or suckers.

So powerful, indeed, is the adhesion that it would be

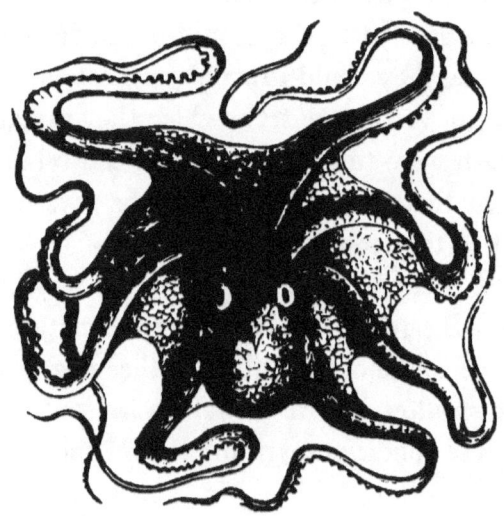

THE OCTOPUS.

easier to tear the sucker from the arm than to loosen its hold. In some of these creatures the adhesive power is increased by a horny claw arising from the centre of the piston.

Even in the comparatively small specimens which are exhibited in our aquaria, the power of suction is almost incredible when compared with the size of the animal. Not long before these lines were written, a curious adventure occurred to an attendant living in an aquarium.

He was employed in the tank which was occupied by the Cuttles, and wore the usual sea-boots, which rise well above the knee. An Octopus (*i.e.*, eight-footed mollusc) which was in the tank, gently thrust out one of its arms and affixed it to a boot. Others followed in succession, attaching themselves imperceptibly like bad habits, until half the arms were fastened to the boot, and the other half to the walls of the tank.

The man tried in vain to detach the suckers which had clung round his boot, or those which were sticking against the wall of the aquarium, and in the end he was obliged to slip off the boot, and leave it to the Octopus. Now, if the same man had been bathing during the flow of the tide, and a similar Octopus had affixed its arms to his legs instead of his boots, nothing could have saved his life.

The largest Cuttle, however, that could be captured alive, is as nothing when compared with the enormous species which haunt the southern seas. What may be the size to which these creature can attain it is hardly possible to say. Even in the northern latitudes, one specimen which was thrown up on the shores of Jutland had arms as thick as a man's thigh, and M. Peron found a great Cuttle whose arms were seven inches in diameter.

The largest example of these enormous molluscs that

has been seen alive and attacked was encountered off the coast of Teneriffe. In the winter of 1861 a French steamer, the *Alecton*, fell in with a great Cuttle disporting itself on the surface of the sea. The men tried to harpoon it, but without success, the harpoon merely slipping through the soft tissues of the body without taking hold. Bullets produced scarcely any more effect, going through the body without seeming to do much injury. One bullet, however, inflicted a wound from which issued a mass of blood and foam, accompanied by a strong musky odour.

Then a rope with a slip-knot was passed over its body, and the men tried to haul it out of the water. The creature, however, tore itself away, leaving a fragment of the end of the body in the noose. The men wanted to lower a boat and chase it, but the captain feared lest they might come to harm against so novel an opponent, and would not give his permission.

The piece that came on board weighed about forty-six pounds, and the officers calculated that the weight of the entire animal, which was about sixteen feet, exceeded four thousand pounds! It was one of the short-armed species, the length of the arms being only five or six feet.

There are some species which have one pair of arms enormously elongated, specimens having been found in which the arms were thirty feet in length, and as thick as a man's wrist. In these animals, the extremity of the arms is flattened like the blade of a paddle, and furnished with suckers of enormous power. Moreover, when the creature has seized its prey with these arms, it can lock them together, and so render escape impossible.

In the southern seas these gigantic molluscs are greatly dreaded by the natives. The long arms can be slid over the edges of the canoe, and if they seized one of the crew, he would certainly lose his life, were he not prepared for such an attack.

These molluscs approach the vertebrate animals in many respects, and especially in their nervous system. The nerves are concentrated near the junction of the arms in such a manner that they form a sort of brain.

EXTREMITY OF ARM.

The natives are aware of this fact, and always keep a long, sharp wooden spike in the boat. When attacked by a Cuttle, they drive the spike into the brain, when the suckers relax their hold, the arms collapse, and the animal dies at once.

They employ the same mode when fishing for Cuttles. They first make a bait which looks anything but a bait to those who do not know its use. It is formed of the large cowry shells of these seas, and is shaped like a buoy. This is tied to a cord and trailed slowly along the bed of the sea. The Cuttle sees it, thinks it to be some living prey, stretches out an arm and attaches some of its two thousand suckers.

The fisherman then gives a sharp pull, when the creature attaches another arm. At last, the Cuttle twines all its arms round its supposed prey and attaches all the suckers that can be brought to bear. Then the fisherman rapidly draws up the line, jerks the Cuttle out of the water before it can loosen its hold, stabs it at the junction of the arms and kills it.

I have no doubt that if a good marksman on board the *Alecton* had known where to aim, he could have killed the gigantic Cuttle with a single bullet.

HOMES UNDER THE SEA.

CHAPTER II.

THE COMMON SEPIA.

A FAMILIAR example of these long-armed Cuttles is to be found on our own shores. It is popularly called the Sepia, and is better known by two of its productions than by its form.

One of these productions is the Cuttle "bone" which is so frequently thrown on our shores after a gale. This structure presents another approach to the vertebrate animals, as it is the first example of an internal skeleton. It lies loosely in a sort of bag, so that when the dead Sepia is eaten by the crabs, shrimps, and other crustacea, the "bone" is detached and floats away. Although made of calcareous substance, it is lighter than water. The chalk is deposited in successive layers connected by delicate ridges, which, when the "bone" is broken, look like rows of little pillars. This structure enables the "bone" to float on the surface of the sea, and its object appears to be to strengthen the body without increasing its weight.

The common slug possesses an internal shell exactly

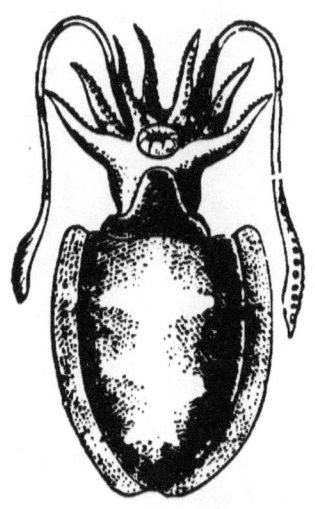

THE COMMON SEPIA.

analogous to that of the Sepia, though not so elaborate in structure.

In the Mediterranean, the Sepia is so plentiful that, after a storm, the Cuttle-bones are heaped up into a ridge several miles in length. The inhabitants of the coast use the animal largely for food, and mostly take it by night, spearing it by the aid of torches.

These "bones" are held in great favour by bird

fanciers, who find that they are even better than sand or gravel as aids to digestion. Tooth-powder is also obtained by the simple process of scraping, and for those who travel much the "Cuttle-bone" is found to be preferable to a box of powder.

Still more useful is the well-known colour called "Sepia," which, when genuine, is obtained from this animal.

All the Cuttle tribe possess an internal bag, or sac, which contains a peculiar black liquid. This liquid can be spurted out at the will of the owner, so that the water

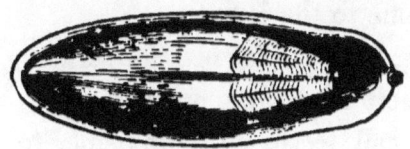

CUTTLE BONE.

around becomes instantly as black as ink. The object of this curious provision is to act as a cover to the creature when it is forced to seek for shelter. If alarmed, it instinctively empties the ink-sac into the water and darts off unperceived.

A gentleman well known in literature once saved his life by recollecting this habit of the Cuttle. He was a good diver, and was amusing himself by fetching up some of the beautiful shells which lay on the sand. Suddenly, a cloud seemed to pass over him, and, on looking up, he saw a large shark hovering over him. He had forgotten to take his long knife with him, as is the custom in these regions, and there was no hope of passing the shark. Under water, especially after being submerged for nearly a minute, there is no time for planning, and the diver gave himself up for lost.

Suddenly, the Sepia's ink-bag flashed across his mind. He dived down again, stirred up the sand with his hands so as to discolour the water, and succeeded in gaining the shore before the shark could find him.

Even in the fossil Sepiæ the ink-bag has been preserved, and a drawing of the fossil animal has been made with its own ink.

Now we come to the jaws.

In the slug, they are formed for scraping rather than masticating, soft food, and are furnished with a great number of small teeth, quite invisible to the unaided eye. But the Cuttles are not only carnivorous but predaceous, and must have jaws which, like those of the lion and tiger or the beak of the eagle, are formed for rending the living flesh.

So, in them, the jaws are modified into a sort of very strong beak, almost exactly like that of a parrot, but much stronger. As the mouth is situated at the junction of the arms, it is evident that the united action of the arms drags the prey into the jaws.

As to the eyes, they are equally modified to suit the habits of the creature.

The slug requires but little sight, and in fact, as it mostly feeds in the dark, could almost do without eyes;

consequently, in the slug they are very small. But the Cuttle needs strong and acute sight, and accordingly the eyes are very large, and are placed upon two prominences, one on either side of the head. These eyes can be seen by referring to the figure of the Octopus on page 32.

Next, we come to the mode of progression. Some of the Cuttles can swim slowly by flapping the arms up and

EGGS OF SEPIA.

down. All of them can crawl by means of the arms, affixing and relaxing the suckers as they advance.

But their chief mode of progress is exactly the same as that which is employed by the larva of the dragon-fly and copied by man in the rocket. Water is taken into a cavity within the body, and expelled with greater or less force according to the will of the animal. At every respiration, the water is taken into the cavity and expelled through a tube called the "siphon." This siphon can be seen in the figure of the Sepia on page 38.

The ink, which has already been mentioned, is also expelled through the siphon.

In some of the Cuttles, popularly known as Squids, the propulsive power is so great that the creatures dart through the water so swiftly that the eye cannot follow them. They can even shoot themselves completely out of the water like the flying-fish, and have often been mistaken for those creatures.

I may mention that a steam vessel has been constructed, which is propelled by the direct action of water in precisely the same way. The engine is called the Hydromotor.

Whether for concealment, or for some unknown object, many of these creatures even exceed the chameleon in the power of changing colour. I have kept both creatures, and have noticed that although the chameleon possesses more positive hues of green and yellow, it does not change so rapidly as the Sepia, over whose body the colours flit as if produced in a magic lantern. The young Sepiæ seem to be in this respect superior to the old, and can be very easily watched.

In the summer, especially after a high wind, clusters of Sepia eggs may be found on the shore. They are black, smooth, and fastened together in such a way that they look exactly like bunches of black grapes. Mostly, their flexible foot-stalks are twisted round the stem of a sea-weed.

If the eggs be placed in a vessel of sea-water, young Sepiæ will generally be hatched from some of the eggs.

As they are lively beings and rapidly consume oxygen, it is better to place them in a wide pan, the water being only just deep enough to cover the eggs.

When hatched, the little Sepiæ are about half an inch in length, and with very short tentacles. As soon as they are hatched, they traverse the vessel and survey it curiously, propelling themselves by means of the siphon. If a layer of sand be at the bottom of the pan, their course can be traced by means of the grooves which each effort of propulsion makes in the sand. When they have taken a leisurely survey of their new home, they hover over one spot, blow out the sand so as to form a cavity, and settle down in it with a curious air of being at home. While they are traversing the pan, they perpetually change colour, and not for two consecutive seconds do they retain the same hue. Like the chameleon, the Sepia continues to change its colour for some time after death. I do not, however, find that Sepiæ assimilate themselves to the colour of surrounding objects, as the chameleon mostly does. Thus we have seen how perfectly, yet how simply, the soft-bodied and helpless mollusc can be transformed into the terror of the seas, and become fierce, active, voracious, and possessing a set of weapons which combine the terrors of the tiger's mighty paw and the lithe coils of the equally terrible boa-constrictor.

HOMES UNDER THE SEA.

CHAPTER III.

SEA STARS OR STARFISHES.

WE have seen how the soft body of the snail or slug can be converted into a terrible instrument of destruction in the previous chapters.

We shall also see how the fragile bodies of the jelly-fishes can overpower the strongest man, and that their fibres, not thicker than the threads of a spider's web, and even more easily broken, bear within their almost invisible filaments a poison apparatus which is as deadly as the fang of the rattlesnake.

The creatures are gifted with these structures for the purpose of enabling them to obtain food, and indeed, if we look to the details of any living being, we shall see that most of them are subordinated to that object.

Now we come to a group of marine creatures in which the food-procuring structure is so remarkable, that if it had not been seen in action no one could have suspected it. Even dissection could have given no clue to it.

There are few marine animals which appear to be so absolutely secured from foes as the bivalve molluscs, such as the oyster, the scallop, the cockle, and the mussel. Their lives appear, according to our ideas, to be peculiarly dull and stupid, but there does seem to be a compensation in their immunity from foes. Among reptiles the slow-moving tortoise presents a somewhat similar combination, but even the box-tortoise itself, which can contract its legs and head within the shell, and then shut itself up like a box, is not nearly so secure as either of these molluscs.

Supposing that a hungry man were supplied with oysters, and forbidden the use of tools with which he could either break the shells or force them open, he would probably starve to death. If we were to be asked to select some inhabitant of the sea which would be best fitted for feeding on oysters, we should naturally search for some large fish, furnished with teeth and jaws powerful enough to crush the firmly-closed shells, for to force them asunder would be almost impossible.

Any of my readers who has opened oysters, knows practically that even with the aid of a knife made expressly for the purpose, a novice in the art finds the greatest difficulty in forcing the shells asunder. He cuts his fingers and breaks the shells, but they still remain obstinately closed.

Now, strange as it may seem, the worst of the oyster's foes destroy it by forcing its shells apart before they eat it, and these foes are popularly known as STAR-FISHES.

The name, by the way, is a very unfortunate one, the

Fig. 1.—FIVE-FINGERED STARFISH.

French word *Etoiles de Mer*, or Sea Stars, being far superior, as it conveys no idea of fish.

With us, the word is used in the loosest possible manner. Oysters, periwinkles, limpets, whelks, lobsters, crabs, and shrimps, are all termed "shell-fish." Then there are the jelly-fishes, and now we have the starfishes. Even the whales are called fish, and when a party goes to hunt seals, they are said to go sealfishing!

Let us take the most common of the starfishes, the

"Five-finger," which is so plentiful on our shores. (See Fig. 1.) Viewed upon the upper surface, it appears as helpless a being as can well be imagined. It is absolutely incapable of resistance or even of struggle to escape. It has no stinging threads like those of the jelly-fishes, and permits itself to be torn or crushed without seeming to know that it is hurt.

Viewed from the under surface, however, it presents a different aspect. (See Fig. 2.)

In the centre of the arms there is an aperture which may do duty for the mouth, but there is not even a semblance of jaws, nor any visible apparatus for taking prey.

Protruding from the whole of the lower surface are many rows of little semi-transparent papillæ, not unlike the "horns" of snails in shape, and each having a little rounded knob at the end. They are in perpetual motion, being continually protruded or withdrawn, and moving in all directions, as if feeling for something.

This, in fact, is the case. Each of these papillæ is an organ of progression, and they are feeling for some object to which they can adhere. The little rounded tip acts as a sucker, and so, when the papillæ are brought into contact with any firm surface, they can cause the creature to advance or recede with a smooth, slow, and gradual motion.

Perhaps the words "advance" and "recede" are hardly applicable to the starfish, as it has no head, no tail, and can move with equal facility in every direction. The technical name for these papillæ is "ambulacra," from the Latin word *ambulare*, to walk.

Their structure is remarkably beautiful, but the mechanical contrivances which render them capable of pro-

Fig. 2.—UNDER SURFACE OF THE FIVE-FINGERED STARFISH.

trusion, retraction, adherence, and detachment, are so complicated that they cannot be easily described. Suffice it to say that along the under surface of the body are a number of hard, shelly shields, set closely side by side, and that these shields are pierced with tiny holes called "ambulacral apertures." Through these apertures the ambulacra pass. How they are worked I will try to explain.

Suppose that a vessel were shaped like an ordinary water carafe, but made of very thin and very elastic india-rubber. Let this vessel be filled with water and the mouth stopped. Now, if the ball be squeezed between the hands, the water will be driven into the neck and cause it to expand.

Suppose that the neck of the vessel were passed through a hole in a thick log of wood, and were only just large enough to fit; it could not expand sideways, and must do so downwards, so as to become lengthened. When the pressure is taken off the ball, the water will return into it, and the neck be drawn back through the hole.

This is just what happens with the starfish, the ambulacrum being represented by the carafe, and the pierced log by the ambulacral plate.

As far as we can see, the starfishes have neither eyes nor organs of scent. Yet they are, in some unknown manner, able to detect the presence of food and to direct themselves towards it.

Every one who has fished in the sea with a bait of whelk or limpet, must often have been annoyed by finding, when they drew in their lines, a starfish fastened on the bait, with its arms clasped tightly round it. Now it is not likely that in these cases the bait has happened to alight in the middle of the starfish, and it is tolerably evident that the creature must have directed its course to its food.

Fishermen when they find a starfish devouring their bait, always tear it asunder and fling the halves into the sea. It is a very foolish thing to do, for, like many animals of low organization, the starfish can reproduce the missing portions, and so each half becomes a separate starfish.

Even if all the rays be torn asunder, each of them will throw out four more arms, and so in process of time look as if nothing had happened to it. An example of this curious faculty is shown in the accompanying illustration, Fig. 3.

Lobsters, as most of us know, can reproduce a missing limb, even when they have lost a claw almost as large as the rest of the body. But if torn asunder they die, the restorative power being limited to the limbs.

An interesting experiment can easily be tried, which will show how well the creature can direct its course.

Put a starfish into shallow sea-water—a rock-pool is the best place—and watch the direction in which it begins to move. Now, place in its course a couple of large stones from one to two inches apart, according to the size of the starfish.

Until it arrives at the narrow passage formed by the stones, it crawls with all its rays widely spread. But, as soon as it comes to the stones, it knows how to act. Without stopping for a moment, it pushes one ray between the stones, and goes quietly gliding on. As the centre of the body approaches the aperture, ray after ray is allowed to trail behind, until one ray is in front, and the four others are pressed closely together behind it.

The mention of the ambulacral plates brings us to the hard structures of the body. The whole under surface of the body is made up of a series of shelly

Fig 3.—STARFISH REPRODUCING MISSING PORTIONS.

plates, largest at the base of the ray, and diminishing gradually in size to the tip. Beside these plates there are successive rows of shelly joints arranged in regular order, and so jointed to the ambulacral plates as to permit the needful amount of flexibility in the rays. There are many hundreds of these pieces in each starfish.

And they are arranged in such exquisite order, and produce such harmony of outline, that their beauty is beyond the power of description. A portion of these plates may be seen in Fig. 1.

That starfishes are destructive to oysters has long been known, but it was thought that in order to reach the oyster the starfish waited until the mollusc opened its shells, and then prevented it from closing them by thrusting one of its rays between them.

Such a process, however, would have been impossible, as the adductor muscle by which the shells are closed is so powerful that the ray would be crushed as soon as the mollusc took alarm. Several instances have been recorded of mice strangled by oysters. The mouse had gained access to a fishmonger's shop, found an oyster with its shells open, and put in its head for the sake of eating the oyster. Directly the mollusc felt the touch of the intruder's teeth, it instinctively closed its shell on the neck of the mouse and so strangled it.

The real mode by which the starfish attacks, opens, and devours the oyster is as follows:—

First, the starfish clasps its arms round the oyster, so as to bring its mouth against the edges of the shells. It is able to hold itself firmly in its place by means of the ambulacra, each of which is a separate sucker.

Then from the mouth it protrudes a series of vesicles, one corresponding to each ray. These vesicles are never equal in size, some being as large as grapes, while the others scarcely equal peas in dimensions.

Whatever may be the nature of the contents of the vesicles, it seems to have the power of penetrating between the shells and paralysing the adductor muscles. The shells are thus forced to open, and the Starfish then pushes the vesicles between them, and absorbs into its own digestive system the whole of the oyster except the adductor muscle.

A French naturalist, who was watching the ebbing tide, observed a number of odd-looking, ruddy balls rolling along as the water receded. On approaching them, he found that each ball was composed of five or six Five-finger Starfishes, all with their rays interlaced. On opening the balls he found that within each of them was a Trough-shell *(Mactra stultorum)*, and that the Starfishes were ranged round it so that their mouths came in contact with the edges of the shells. In every case the shells were slightly open.

It might be thought that by dissection a keen observer might have detected the deadly vesicles; but no sooner is the Starfish detached from its prey than the vesicles collapse, and, large as they were when dilated, leave not the slightest trace of their existence.

HOMES UNDER THE SEA.

CHAPTER IV.

WHAT ARE THE STARFISHES?

WE may now ask ourselves a few natural questions. What are the Starfishes; what is their place in zoology, and what is their life history?

In the first place they form one of the two sections of a great and important group of animals which are scientifically termed Echinodérmata, *i.e.* Hedgehog-skinned, and which comprise the Starfishes and Sea Urchins.

This group appears at first sight to be completely isolated, and to have no relationship to beings of evidently lower organization on the one side, and of higher organization on the other. Yet, when closely examined, there is perhaps no group which shows more clearly its

Fig. 1.—ENCRINITES, OR LILY-STONES.

mutual relations with lower and higher beings, or which is more important in systematic zoology.

The Echinodérmata, then, form a connected series of links between the Polyps on the one side and the Worm tribe on the other. We shall only be able to trace the links backwards towards the Polyps, leaving those which connect the Starfish with the Worms to another opportunity.

The reader will find the corals described in another chapter, and several figures illustrating the structure of the Polyps that deposit the various corals and madrepores. These Polyps are composed of a stem and stalk, surmounted by a crown of radiating tentacles like the petals of a dahlia.

Now, supposing we have the footstalk greatly elongated, and that the earthy particles, instead of being placed outside the animal, as with the corals and madrepores, are deposited within its tissues, we shall have an approach to a skeleton. Even if the animal were to die and decay, the earthy particles would still remain, and would, under some circumstances, retain the general form of the animal in which they were deposited.

We should then have a stony footstalk surmounted by a crown of stony tentacles.

Let us now take another step.

It is evident that such a creature would be unable to live, as it would be without flexibility, and would be snapped asunder by any movement of the water in which it lived. But, supposing that the earthy particles were deposited in a series of solid pieces, and each piece connected with the others by the soft parts, we should have a creature which was mostly composed of stony matter, and yet was perfectly flexible.

Fig. 2.—COMATULA, OR FEATHER STAR.

Such a structure is to be found in the remarkable beings called Encrinites.

In the former ages of the earth, Encrinites existed in

the greatest profusion, and their fossil remains are so plentiful that they are known by the popular name of Lily-Stones, and indeed were long thought to be petrified lilies. The word Encrinite has a similar signification. The variegated marble which is so much used for mantelpieces is composed almost entirely of Encrinites, and the loose joints of the stem are well known as Saint Cuthbert's beads.

At the present age of the earth, the Encrinites, having done the work for which they were made, have become almost extinct. It is interesting, however, to remark, that one species has been discovered in a living state on our coasts. It is called *Pentacrinus Europæus*, and a magnified portrait of it is given. It is a very little creature, not much more than half an inch in length; but in science mere size is of very trifling consideration. The word Pentracrinus signifies five-sided Encrinite, and is given to it because its coronet is composed of five double rays. (Fig. 1.)

Each of these flowers is capable of extending or contracting its petal-like rays, and sweeping food into the central mouth.

Now, supposing that the flower could be detached from the stem, and instead of merely waving backwards and forwards, should be able to creep at liberty, we should find a sort of Starfish.

Such a Starfish exists plentifully, and is well known under the name of *Comátula*, or Feather Star.

These creatures, of which there are many species, are

evidently the lowest of their group. The structure is almost exactly like that of the *Encrinus, i.e.* a number of stony pieces deposited within the soft tissues, and connected by them so as to possess flexibility. (Fig. 2.)

Fig. 3.—GORGONOCEPHALUS, OR GORGON'S HEAD.

By far the greater bulk of the creature is composed of these earthy pieces, and, as is the case with the Encrinite, from each of the principal rays project a series of secondary rays, each being formed of a number of joints capable of movement. These secondary rays seem to subserve the same purpose as the ambulacra of the higher Starfishes, and to act as means of locomotion.

Next we come to a remarkable creature, popularly called the Sea Basket, and scientifically known as *Gorgonocéphalus*, or Gorgon's Head.

In this animal we have a decided advance, the various parts being connected, not by a mere semi-glutinous tissue, but by a tough skin. (Fig. 3.)

Each of the five rays of this creature subdivides close to the body into two, each of these into two more, and so on. The subdivided rays become smaller and smaller in proportion to their number, until we find more than eighty thousand delicate fibres at their tips.

The Gorgonocéphalus crawls by means of these tendril-like extremities of the arms, just as does the Comatula with its secondary rays. When it feeds, it envelops its prey within its multitudinous arms, and so conveys the food to its mouth.

The next advance is to be found in the creatures called Brittle Stars, or Snake-tailed Starfishes. Their scientific name is *Ophiócoma*, *i.e.* Snake-haired, or *Ophiúrus*, *i.e.* Snake-tail. (Fig. 4.)

They derive their name of Brittle Stars from the fact that, like many of the higher creatures, when they are alarmed they can break themselves into several pieces. The blindworm, for example, can throw off its tail, and the lobster can shake off any of its limbs. But the Brittle Stars can simply shatter themselves to pieces,

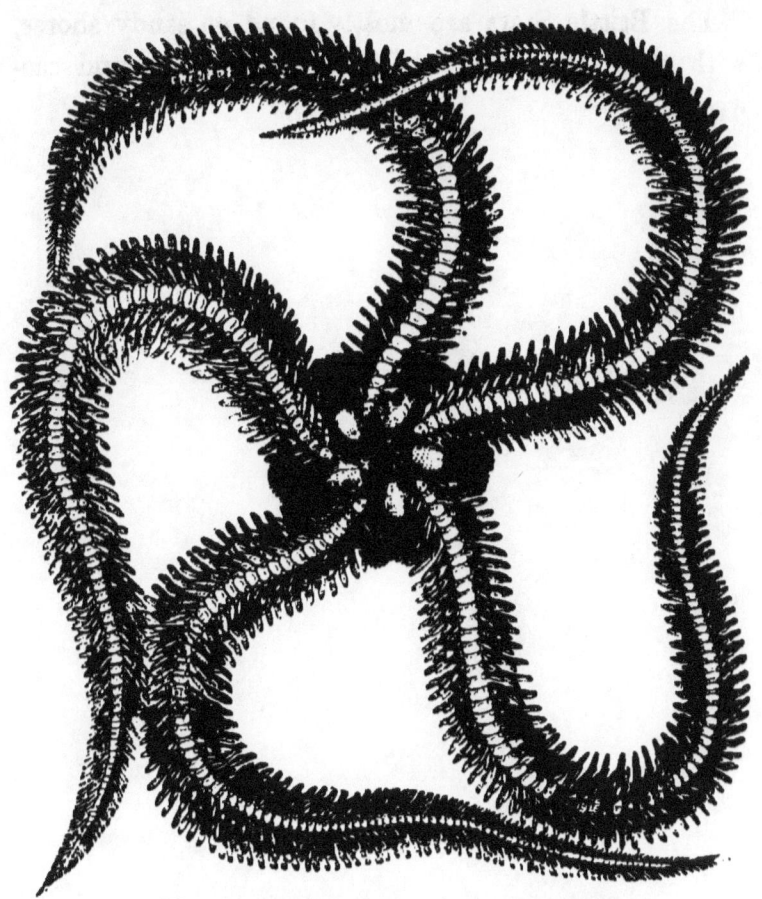

Fig. 4.—BRITTLE STARS, OR SNAKE-TAIL.

leaving nothing but the small central disk. Consequently it is no easy matter to obtain a perfect specimen. Professor Forbes tells a ludicrous story of his discomfiture by a Brittle Star, which rapidly dissolved itself into fragments, and winked derisively at him with the eye-like mouth in the centre of the disk.

The Brittle Stars are mostly found on sandy shores, with their long and flexible rays twined round sea-weeds.

HOMES UNDER THE SEA.

CHAPTER V.

SEA URCHINS.

THE Starfishes, as we have shown, form a series of links which connect the polypes with the worms. The Five-finger, or Cross Fish, as it is sometimes called, seems to be the central link of the chain.

The next link towards the higher beings is easily found.

Supposing that the skin of a Five-finger could be flattened and extended as far as the tips of the rays, just as the web of a duck's foot extends between the toes, we should have a creature which, retaining the five rays, their ambulacra, and the mouth in the centre, is yet indicative of another type of form.

Such a creature is found in the Bird's Foot Starfish

(*Palmipes membranaceus*), which can be obtained by the dredge on most of our coasts, but is seldom cast upon the

Fig. 1.—SEA URCHIN.

shore. It is, by the way, a most beautiful being as far as colour goes, the general hue being light yellow, with scarlet lines running along the rays and continued round the edges of the connecting membrane.

Next, let us imagine that the calcareous skeleton, instead of being composed of movable parts, be soldered together, so that the rays can no longer be bent, we shall have the Cake Urchin, or Shield Urchin (*Echinarachnius*), so called on account of its flatness.

For the next step, let us suppose that before the change of skeleton takes place, the Bird's Foot Starfish were rolled up, so as to bring the tips of the rays in contact, we should have a creature which is well known as the common Sea Urchin or Sea Egg (*Echinus*).

In these creatures ambulacra still retain their places, but are not nearly so conspicuous as in the Starfishes, especially as they are nearly hidden by the remarkable appendages which have earned for the creatures the title of Sea Urchins or Hedgehogs.

The whole external surface of the Sea Urchin is covered with radiating spines very much resembling those of the hedgehog, but having a much more complex mechanism, and being capable of movement in any direction. How they are moved, we shall now see.

We are all familiar with the "ball-and-socket" joint, which is so much used in machinery. Carrying out what I believe to be an universal rule, that all mechanical inventions of men have their prototypes in Nature, the spines of the Echinus afford an absolutely perfect example of the ball-and-socket joint.

Upon nearly the whole external surface of the Sea

Urchin are set rows of globular projections, varying in size and number according to the species.

Upon these projections are set the calcareous spines, each of which is furnished at the base with a hemispherical cup, a very little larger than the ball to which it belongs. A muscle surrounds both ball and socket, serving the double purpose of fastening them together and of moving the spine in any required direction.

In the Mamillated Urchin, a figure of which is here

Fig. 2.—MAMILLATED URCHIN STRIPPED OF ITS SPINES.

given, the spines are comparatively few, but of enormous dimensions. Species of similar Urchins are very common in a fossil state, and go by various popular names. So large are the spines of several species now inhabiting the tropical seas, that, when calcined, they form excellent slate-pencils.

In our common Sea Urchins, the spines are very numerous, and very small, slender, and pointed. Being also brittle, they must not be handled roughly, as they are apt to pierce the hand and then snap off, so that they cannot be extracted without the use of the knife.

In the Cake Urchins they are short, and as fine as human

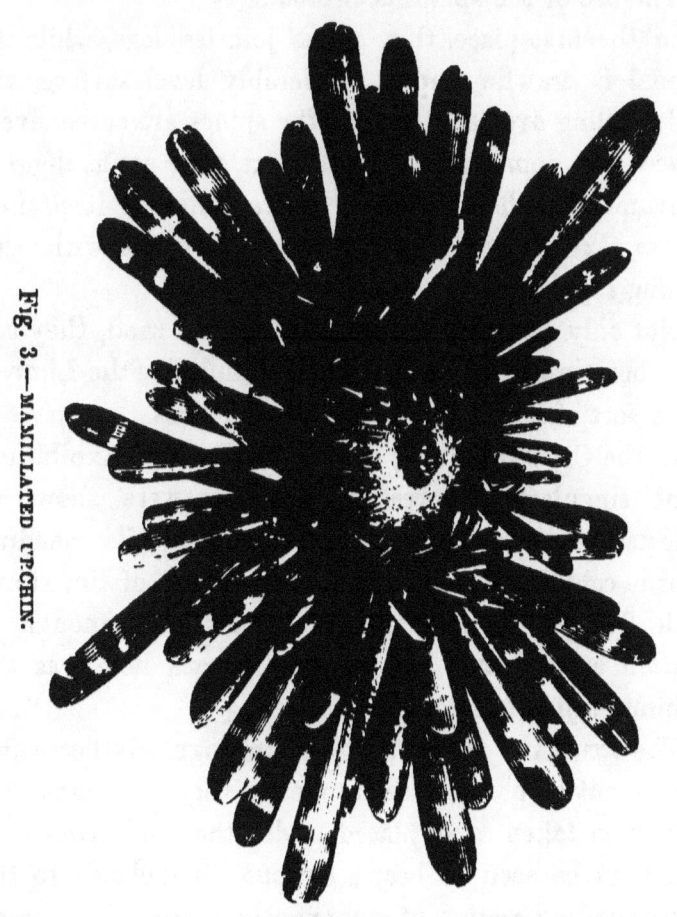

Fig. 3.—MAMILLATED URCHIN.

hair. Yet each of them has its own ball-and-socket joint with the corresponding muscle, and, when viewed under the microscope, each is seen to be formed of a number of rings edged with radiating spinclets. The common "mare's tail" of our streams will give a good idea of the shape of a Cake Urchin spine.

The use of the spines is twofold.

In the first place, they act as jointless legs, while the animal is crawling upon a tolerably level surface, the body rolling over and over as the spines are successively raised and depressed. In the next, they act as digging instruments, whereby the creature can sink itself into the sand; an operation which it performs with surprising rapidity.

Not only can they scoop holes in the sand, they can even bore into hard rock. The Echinus, like the Limpet, has a sort of home in which it usually lives.

In the Crystal Palace, during the Electric Exhibition, some singularly interesting specimens were shown of objects that were brought to the surface while mending marine cables. Among them was a block of limestone, with five or six hemispherical holes large enough to contain an ordinary orange, and in each hole was the Echinus which had scooped it.

The structure of these spines is singularly beautiful, but cannot be properly seen unless a very thin transverse section is taken, and placed under the microscope. It will then be seen to bear a curious resemblance to the corresponding section of any exogenous tree. The spine of the porcupine presents a very similar appearance.

Should the creature wish to climb a rock, the spines would be useless. It therefore has to make use of the ambulacra, just as the Starfish does. These wonderful instruments of locomotion are kept within the body until they are wanted, and then they are protruded as they are wanted. As they must necessarily pass beyond the spines, they are of considerable length when extended to the utmost.

Generally the Echinus prefers to use those ambulacra which are situated round the mouth. If specimens be kept in an aquarium, they will move freely about, and it is a very interesting sight to watch them gliding along

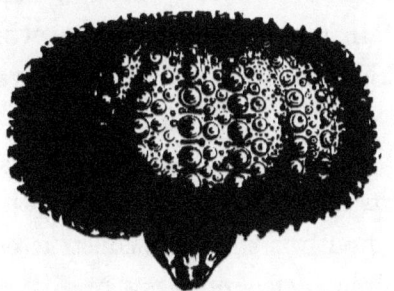

Fig. 4.—SHELL OF SEA URCHIN.

the glass with a movement almost as slow and regular as that of the minute-hand of a watch.

The apertures through which they pass are best seen by opening the shell, holding it up to the light, and looking at it from the interior. They can be very well distinguished, looking like rows of very fine needle-holes. Even in the largest specimens these holes are exceedingly minute. The mechanism of the ambulacra themselves is precisely the same as has been described in another chapter.

The mouth having been mentioned in connection with the ambulacra, we will examine its structure.

Judging by that of the Starfishes, to which the Urchins are so closely allied, we might naturally expect to see a similar structure. But, in the Echini, we find a form of mouth so widely distinct from that of the Starfishes, that it seems as if it belonged to a totally distinct group of animals.

As the reader may remember, the mouth of the Starfish is simply an aperture at the junction of the rays, without either teeth or jaws. Through this aperture are protruded certain membranous vesicles, which have the power of sucking an oyster or other bivalve from its shell.

The Echinus would not be able to feed after this fashion. It has no flexible rays wherewith to grasp its prey, and the mouth is therefore constructed on a totally different principle. It is not easy to give a full description of this wonderful apparatus without more diagrams than can be accommodated within our limits.

If the reader will refer to Fig. 4, he will see a conical projection below, formed of several pointed pieces. In Fig. 5, where the Echinus is shown in section, the same projection is shown, together with its continuation into the interior. Altogether, there are five of these pieces, corresponding, like the ambulacral apertures, with the five rays. Fig. 5 shows three of these rays, with the apertures slightly indicated.

Again referring to Fig. 4, the reader will see that the

points are distinct from the portion immediately above them. In the actual object, the distinction is very conspicuous, the points being shining white, while the upper portions are dead greyish white. These latter are seen within the shell in Fig. 5, two being shown in full, and a portion of a third behind them. Their round points are the tips of the real teeth, and the dull white structures are the sheaths in which the teeth work.

Now we come to a curious and unexpected analogy

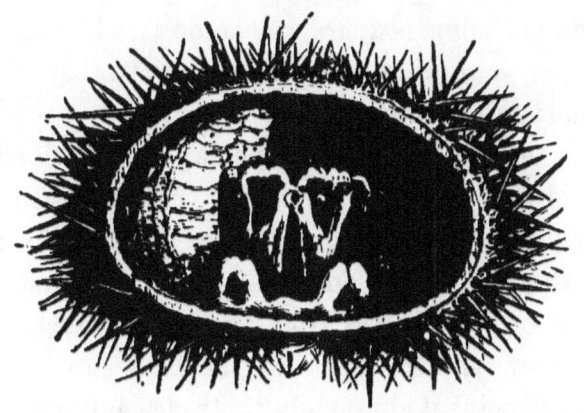

Fig. 5.—SECTION OF SEA URCHIN.

between the teeth of the Echinus and those of the rabbit, rat, or any other rodent animal.

In the rodent, the gnawing teeth are very long and curved, and are almost entirely buried in the jaw, only their tips projecting from the bone. So are those of the Echinus, the sheath taking the place of the jaw.

In the rodent, the teeth are very much harder than the jaw in which they are set, and in the Echinus the teeth are very much harder than the sheath in which they play.

In the rodent, the teeth are constantly worn away at the tips, fresh tooth matter being formed at the bases. Precisely the same provision of nature is found in the teeth of the Urchins.

Now, however, we find ourselves face to face with a curious mechanical problem.

In the rodent, the upper jaw is fixed and the lower jaw moves up and down, carrying the teeth with it; but in the radiated animals there can be no jaw like that of a vertebrate, and so there must be some other mode of comminuting the food.

On examining the dental apparatus more closely, we shall find that instead of being fixed in the sheath, as the rodent tooth is fixed in the jaw, the sheath is fixed, and the tooth slides up and down in it. Suppose that we cut off three or four inches from the tip of a scimitar or curved sabre sheath, and draw the blade up and down so that the point is alternately protruded and withdrawn, we shall see how the tooth of the Urchin is worked.

To each tooth is fixed a double set of very powerful muscles, the stronger serving to pull the tooth downwards, and the weaker to draw it upwards.

Another point now comes before us.

There are five of these chisel-like teeth, all passing through a circular aperture, and meeting together at their tips. Now, if we were to set five ordinary chisels in like manner, they could not meet at their tips, and there would be a pentagonal opening in the centre. But if we were to grind away the angles of the tips, keeping the edges still sharp, we should have just such an apparatus as is shown in Fig. 4.

The five teeth and their corresponding sheaths are so firmly bound together by the muscles and ligaments, that the entire apparatus can be easily removed without separating its constituent parts. The whole of this framework is bound to the interior of the Urchin by means of ligaments which are attached to five strong staples made of the same calcareous matter as that of which the shell is composed. These staples are set round the orifice through which the teeth protrude, and are shown in Fig. 5.

After the death of the animal decay rapidly sets in, so that if the shell be broken the entire dental framework falls out. This framework is often found on the sea-shore, and is popularly known by the name of "Aristotle's Lantern."

HOMES UNDER THE SEA.

CHAPTER VI.

SEA URCHINS—MATERIAL AND DEVELOPMENT.

THERE is yet another point in the structure of these wonderful beings, the Sea Urchins, which we must consider.

They may be found of all sizes, from that of a pea to that of a melon. They retain the same shape throughout their lives, and therefore must have some means of increasing in size with absolute regularity. The solution of this problem may readily be found by opening the Urchin and looking at the inside of the shell. Thus the structure will then be seen to consist of hexagonal plates, two sides being very much longer than the others. Each plate is slightly hollowed. The interior of the shell is lined with a membrane which passes between the plates and secretes the calcareous matter of which they are composed. Additional material is constantly added to the *edges* of the plates, so that the growth of the entire structure must necessarily be equable in every direction, and its shape preserved unaltered. These hexagonal plates are slightly indicated in Fig. 5 (page 71).

A similar provision for equal growth may be seen in the shell of a common tortoise, the concentric lines showing the manner in which the additional material has been deposited.

On some of our coasts, and especially in the Channel Islands, the Urchin is used as food. At the proper season of the year, the interior is almost entirely filled with eggs. These Urchins are boiled, and go by the popular name of Sea Eggs.

One of the most interesting points in the life history of these creatures is the mode of their development. When hatched from the egg, they bear as little resemblance to their perfect form as a caterpillar does to the brilliant insect into which it will in time be changed.

All these animals, whether Starfishes, or Urchins, or Holothures, assume, when they first issue from the egg, a form so totally unlike that of their parents, that only of late years has their real status been known. The young of the Starfishes and Urchins had long been known to naturalists under the name of *Pluteus*, and are so similar in form that the description of one will answer very fairly for the other.

About August or September, according to the warmth of the season, the water is full of these Plutei. They are scarcely distinguishable to the unassisted eye, partly on account of their transparency, and partly by reason of their minute size, which scarcely exceeds the thirty-sixth of an inch in diameter.

Their shape is very remarkable, and not easy of description.

Let the reader try to imagine a wooden office-stool standing on four long diverging legs. Then, let there be four rods rather longer than the legs, screwed into the edges of the seat, and diverging much farther than the legs, so that their ends are off the ground. Then let there be two short rods fixed to the under part of the seat and pointing downwards, and two rather longer rods fixed to the upper edge of the seat and pointing upwards and outwards. Lastly, let a much thicker rod be fixed into the middle of the seat and point directly upwards. This will give some idea of the form of the Pluteus, which has sometimes been compared to the framework of a skeleton clock.

Now for its material.

Change the whole of the stool, legs, and rods into glass, except the seat. Let this be of white chalk, and let a thread of the same material run up the centres of the rods nearly as far as their tips. Strange as it may seem, this is the appearance of the Pluteus when viewed under a microscope.

During this phase of existence, the Pluteus enjoys considerable power of locomotion.

SEA URCHINS—MATERIAL AND DEVELOPMENT. 77

There are many aquatic creatures which, when adult, are either fixed to one spot, or, at all events, can move but slowly, and yet, when in their preliminary stages of

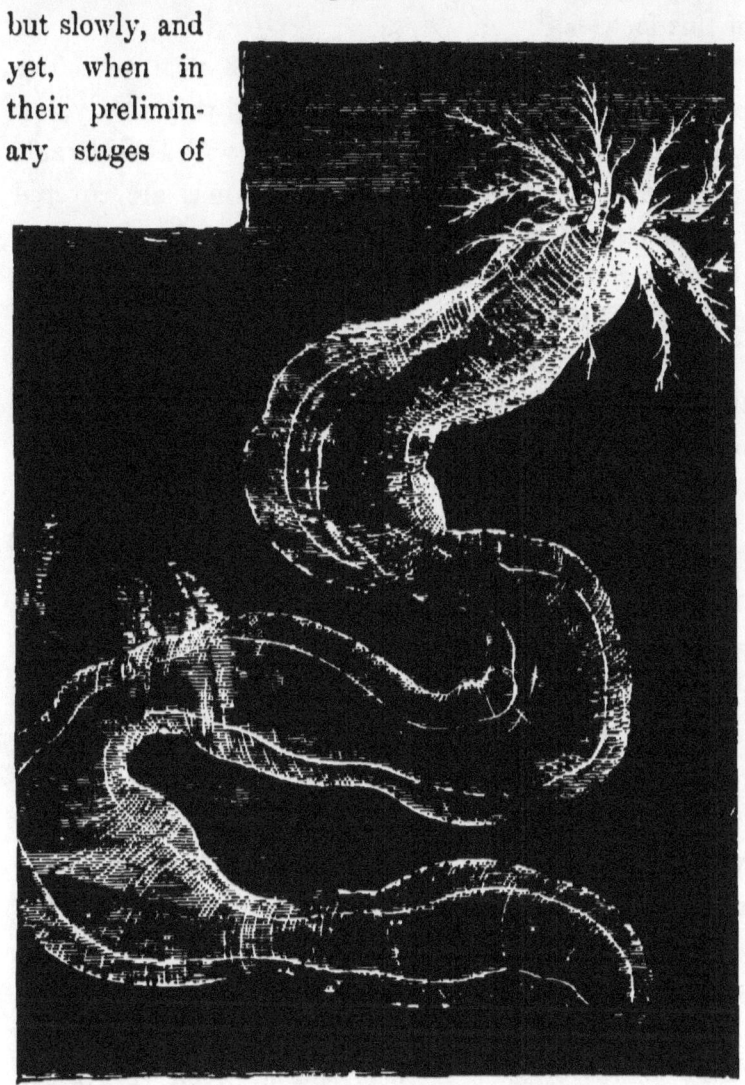

Fig. 6.—SYNAPTA.

existence, are able to move at will through the water. The sponges, barnacles, and oysters are familiar examples of this fact.

We find the same phenomena in these creatures. The perfect Starfish or Urchin can only crawl very slowly, but when it was a Pluteus, it could swim with considerable rapidity. The long arms of the Pluteus are covered with cilia, which, by their regular and successive vibrations, drive the animal through the water.

As the little creature proceeds in development, the centre increases in thickness and density, the arms, with their cilia, gradually disappear, their place being taken by spines and ambulacra, and so the swimming Pluteus becomes a crawling Urchin.

We now come to the last group of Echinoderms, showing how they are linked to the worms.

On reference to the illustrations, Figs. 6 and 7, the reader will see two remarkable objects, each having a tuft of tentacles at one end. These are Synaptas, a species of Holothure, and are chosen because in general form they approach the worms.

The Holothures are found in most of the warmer seas, and many of them are highly valued as food, under the name of Trepang, Sea Slug, or Sea Cucumber.

They are prepared for sale by being boiled, pressed and dried, and differ greatly in their value. To an unskilled eye they are scarcely more inviting than so many scraps of shoe leather, and all look very much alike. Yet all are important articles of commerce, and while one will cost but a penny or two, another, to all appearance exactly like it, can be sold for its weight in silver.

Fig. 7.—SYNAPTA.

In the British Museum there is a fine collection of the various qualities of Trepang. In these creatures the body is much elongated, and, instead of being covered with calcareous plates and spines, has no real spines, and only a few very small thin plates round the mouth. To these plates are attached the muscles which enable the creature to lengthen or shorten its body. The ambulacra, however, are retained, and by their presence show that the creature belongs to the same group as the Starfish and Urchin.

Round the mouth is placed a set of feathery tentacles, which are used in procuring food.

A few years ago, I think in 1878 or 1879, some fishermen who were trawling in the Bay of Halifax, Nova Scotia, found in their net a creature which they did not know. At first they dubbed it a Devil Fish, but at last decided that it was a mermaid. They dared not touch it, but towed it into Halifax, where it was publicly exhibited as a living mermaid. A lady actually told me that she had seen it, and that it had a face, arms, and hands like those of a human being.

I wrote to a friend at Halifax, and then learned, to my great amusement, that the "mermaid" was nothing but a large Holothure which had been brought by the Gulf Stream.

These Holothures possess a very singular habit.

When they are alarmed, or otherwise discomposed, they will throw off their crown of tentacles, and empty their bodies of all the internal organs, including the stomach. They will then lie in a perfectly quiescent state for several months, at the expiration of which time they will have grown a new crown of tentacles and a fresh set of internal organs. Sometimes the creature will go still further, and, by violently contracting the body in several places, will actually cut itself into pieces.

The Synaptas exhibit a beautiful set of appendages to the skin. They are, however, so minute that their forms cannot be seen without the aid of a microscope.

The skin is nearly covered with little tubercles, and upon the tubercles are set a number of transparent spicules formed almost exactly like the anchors used by the ancients. The shank of the anchor is affixed to a little shield composed of the same material, which is pierced with holes arranged so as to produce a definite pattern.

Each species of Synapta has its own pattern of anchor and shield, so that a collection of them forms a singularly interesting set of microscopic objects.

The object of these tiny appendages is at present a total mystery. Their very presence shows that they must subserve some use, and the elaborate care with which they are formed shows that the use must be an important one. But Creation is so large, and man is so small, that a nebula of the skies and a spicule of the Synapta are equally beyond man's grasp, the one from its immeasurable magnitude, and the other from its extreme minuteness.

SOME WONDERS OF THE SEA.

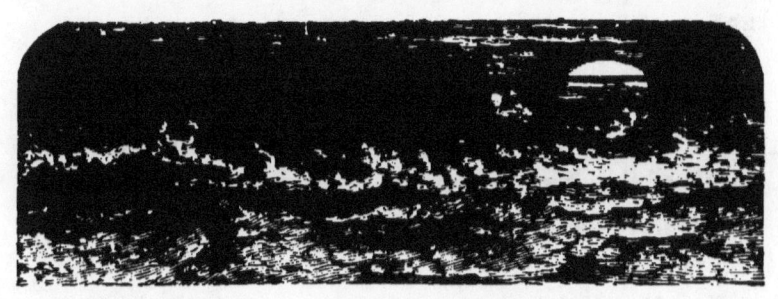

SOME WONDERS OF THE SEA.

CHAPTER I.

JELLY FISHES.

FLUNG upon the sea-shore by the retiring waves, we find lying upon our coast innumerable variously-shaped, helpless, and apparently lifeless lumps of semi-transparent, gelatinous objects, which we call by the popular name of Jelly Fishes, and which are amongst the most beautiful of the many things of beauty with which the Creator has filled His marvellous creation.

Apparently they are nothing but sea-water entangled among a sort of web of animal matter; and, if the largest of them be allowed to dry in the sunshine, it will gradually be dissipated before the hot rays, and a mere pinch of animal matter will constitute its sole remains; indeed, it has been said, and with some truth, that when once a farmer near to the sea-shore carted whole waggon-loads of Jelly Fishes away as manure for his fields, the result of the day's labours in procuring animal substance might have been carried away in one of the pockets of the farmer's coat.

Yet, if we pick up one of these apparently inanimate lumps of jelly, and carry it to a clear pool left by the tide, new life seems to awaken in it. From the edge of the mushroom-like cap a number of delicate transparent filaments are unfolded, and the whole of the cap begins to pulsate slowly, but regularly, the alternate contractions and expansions serving to propel it gently through the water, in which it floats as a parachute floats in the air. It does not seem able to direct its course to any definite point, but it is far from being the inanimate jelly which it appears when lying on the shore.

If taken up in the hands it can be torn, or rather broken, to pieces, the fracture being very much like that of the gelatine which is so often imposed on us under the name of calf's-foot jelly.

Were it only composed of water entangled in a fine animal network, the water would escape when it was broken. But no more water issues from it than when it was intact, and, on holding the broken piece up to the light, fine thread-like network can be seen plainly, as the fibres, which are scarcely thicker than the filaments of a spider's web, have a slightly different refractive power from the water, which is abundantly and securely imprisoned among them.

JELLY FISHES.

Two forms of Jelly Fishes are usually found on our coasts. One form has the simple umbrella, with an edging of very fine transparent filaments, and some flap-like

Fig. 1.—UMBRELLA JELLY FISH.

appendages hanging from the centre; and the other has a narrower and deeper umbrella, with a thick mass of central appendages suspended from it. These latter are called by the generic name of Rhizostoma, or Root-mouthed. Figs. 1 and 2 exhibit examples of the first form, and Figs. 3 and 4 (see pages 95 and 99) represent two species belonging to the second type.

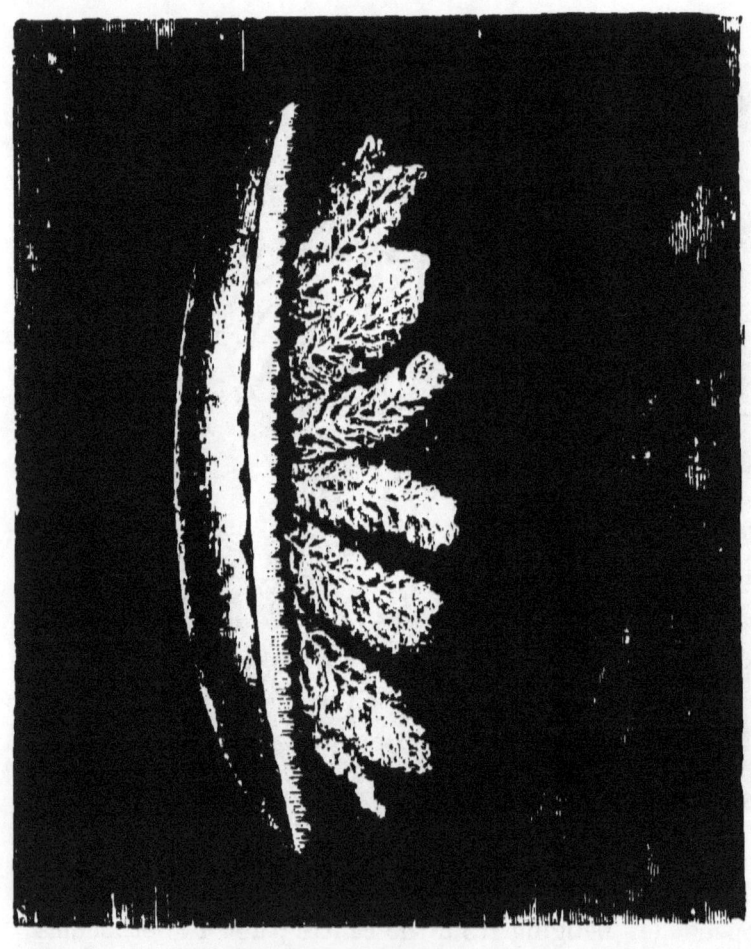

Fig. 2.—UMBRELLA JILLY FISH.

Here I may say that although our knowledge of these wonderful and interesting forms of animal life has greatly increased of late years, so much yet remains to be learned about them that any attempt at their systematic arrangement, and consequently their nomenclature, must be considered as merely provisional.

Suppose that we pick out a small and uninjured specimen, and bring it home for a closer examination. It can be fairly seen in any basin filled with clear sea-water; but as some of its structures require the light to pass among and through them before they can be distinguished, a glass vessel should be used if it can be obtained.

There are always several pastrycooks' shops at a seaside watering-place, and the proprietor will mostly lend on hire to a customer one of the large cylindrical biscuit-glasses. Bell glasses can mostly be obtained, but they almost always have a greenish tinge, which destroys the beauty of the Jelly Fishes placed in them.

Here, then, is our jar of clear sea-water, and in it is a Jelly Fish.

The first point which will strike the observer will be the pulsations of the disc. It continually expands and contracts, as if it were the heart of some creature much higher in the scale of nature.

How and why does it pulsate ?

As far as we know, one of the objects of the pulsation is to allow as much water as possible to pass over the various organs, much as a fish, by perpetually opening and closing its mouth and gill-covers, impels the water over the respiratory apparatus. At one time it was thought that the pulsation of the disc was intended to aid respiration, and that the animal used its respiratory apparatus for the purpose of locomotion. Hence these creatures were called Pulmogrades, *i.e.* moving by means of lungs. The movements, however, are so slow, and the force exerted is so slight, that the animal is unable to stem the feeblest current, and even the largest specimens may be seen borne along by the tide without the slightest attempt to shape a course of their own.

Some few years ago I was much struck with this fact.

I was standing at the end of Southend pier, watching the tide come in. It is an admirable spot for such purpose, as it is a full mile from the shore, and the spectator can see everything that floats in the water beneath him. On that particular day, it was just after half tide, and in consequence all the animal life came from the sea. The water was full of Jelly Fishes, especially those of the Rhizostoma genus, many of which were so large that they seemed to have journeyed from the tropics.

Despite their size, however, and their apparently powerful pulsation, the largest of them were rolled along by the flowing tide as helplessly as the smallest, and not one of them showed the least symptom of intellect enough to determine upon any definite course, or ability to pursue it. A few hours later, when the tide was on the ebb, I returned to the same spot, and there saw the Jelly Fishes borne back with the tide, just as helpless to stay their progress to the sea as they had been to prevent their journey up the river.

Why the pulsation occurs is therefore a mystery. If it be for the purpose of breathing, we can as yet find no respiratory organs. If it be for propulsion, it seems quite inadequate to its office; circulation there is none that can be detected, and so we are driven to the acknowledgment of our ignorance.

How the pulsation is effected is equally a mystery. It is easy enough to say that "the disc is composed of innumerable polyhedral hyaline cells capable of contractile efforts." But that is no explanation. We want to know *how* the disc is able to keep up these pulsations, though possessing neither muscular nor nervous fibres, and as yet no one has been able to discover the secret. The fact is known to every child who visits the sea-shore and uses his eyes, but the wisest man cannot explain it.

There is another function, besides that of movement, which is possessed by many of these Jelly Fishes, namely, the power of stinging. This property was noticed by the ancient naturalists, who gave to the Jelly Fish the names of Acalephæ, *i.e.* nettles, or Medusæ, because the long trailing filaments were venomous as the snakes in Medusa's hair.

Evidently intended for the purpose of paralyzing prey, the poison-threads of the Medusæ are sufficiently venomous to cause intense suffering even to man, and in some cases endanger his life. It is not only the pain inflicted which constitutes the danger, but the effect on the heart and respiratory muscles. The heart seems to cease from beating, and the lungs cannot be inflated. All power goes out of the body and limbs, so that the sufferer becomes helpless for a time, and if in the water might be drowned.

Such, at least, has been my own experience, though persons with a differently constituted nervous organisation might not suffer so severely. The reader may remember that when Captain Webb was making the arrangements for his wonderful swim across the Channel, his chief fear was lest he might be stung by a Jelly Fish. Even though he was protected by a coating of porpoise-oil, he was once slightly stung, but the oil evidently must have partly neutralised the poison, Indeed, after being stung, the most effectual remedies are oil applied externally and brandy taken internally.

As is the case with those who are bitten by venomous snakes, the spirits seem to have no effect whatever on the brain of the sufferer, but only keep up the nervous power until the venom is eliminated from the system.

SOME WONDERS OF THE SEA.

CHAPTER II.

JELLY FISH'S POISONOUS STING.

IT may seem strange that beings of so low an organisation should possess so terrible a power, and we naturally search for the means that it employs.

After a human body has been stung, the surface is covered with the finest imaginable red lines, each line representing the track of the poison-thread. When examined with the help of a magnifying glass, the lines resolve themselves into rows of minute dots, as if tattooed with a needle dipped in carmine, each spot denoting a separate sting.

Now, if we take a single poison-filament and place it under the microscope, a wonderful sight is presented to us.

Although the filament is not thicker than an ordinary spider's thread, it is seen to be studded throughout its length with little oval cells, or capsules, looking like very transparent white grapes. Now, take an object glass of considerable power, not less than half-inch, and examine a single cell.

Here I may mention that throughout this short history of the Medusæ, I spare the reader a mass of scientific terms, certainly very imposing in appearance, but conveying very few ideas. So I shall lay aside " cnidæ," "ecthoræe," "nematocysts," &c., which are the shorthand, so to speak, of zoology, and employ their equivalents in English. They are invaluable to science, because they can be introduced unchanged into any language, and I shall employ such terms as "poison-threads,' "thread-cells," and so forth.

On examining a single cell, its surface appears to be crossed and re-crossed with extremely fine lines of a slightly darker colour than the body of the cell. A careful manipulation of the light and delicate focussing will show that this appearance is caused by a very fine thread coiled up within the cell. Around the base of the cell is a series of tiny hooklets, which remind the entomologists of the beautiful hook-rows which are found in the wings of bees, wasps, ants, and other insects belonging to the same order.

Here, then, is the poison apparatus, and the mode of its action is as follows.

As soon as one of these cells touches any object, the

walls give way, and the poison-thread is shot out to a wonderful distance, its base still remaining attached to

Fig. 3.—RHIZOSTOMA, OR ROOT-MOUTHED.

the cell whence it sprang. Supposing the cell to be as large as an ordinary grape, the thread would be six feet or more in length, and as elastic as the hair-spring of a watch.

What a startling paradox is here! These creatures really seem to exhibit in themselves the two extremes of organisation, their structure appearing to the eye to be scarcely removed above inanimate jelly, and yet, under the microscope, exhibiting a poison-apparatus far surpassing the sting of the bee, wonderful and complicated as it is. Moreover, the bee has only a single sting, while the poison-cells of the Medusæ may be reckoned by myriads.

What may be the nature of this poison we do not at present know. Some persons have thought that it was electric in its nature, and connected with the brilliant phosphorescent powers possessed by many of the species. Its effect on the nervous system strengthens this opinion, and it is certain that no substance known to be poisonous has been discovered. The extremely minute dimensions of the capsules, however, seem to prohibit even chemistry, or its new ally the spectroscope, from a thorough investigation of the cell contents.

Ordinarily, the threads hang at no great length from the disc, as may be seen by reference to Fig. 1. But the Medusæ seem to be able to project the threads to extraordinary distances. At the time when I was so severely stung the Medusa was not within several yards, and though I was swimming leisurely towards it, my feet were struck before my hands. On lifting my arms out of the water, the delicate filaments could easily be seen hanging from the arm like so many spider-threads.

One fact that militates against the electric theory is, that the poison-threads do not depend for action upon the will of the creature to which they belong. If a single filament be separated and be washed against the human skin, it will sting with as much virulence as if it were still attached to the body whence it sprung, and which may be miles away.

This I have personally experienced. I seem to have a particular attraction for the terrible "Stinger" or "Stanger" of our coasts (*Cyanea*); and if a single filament should happen to be floating about when I am in the water, it is sure to find me. I have been stung even in an enclosed swimming-bath on the Devonshire coast, an almost invisible fibre having been introduced into the bath through the supply pipe.

Now we will turn to the umbrella-like disc, and shall find that it is by no means the homogeneous lump of jelly that it appears to be when carelessly inspected.

Look at any one of them as it lies on the sea-shore, and you will see four rings of darker substance than the rest of the disc. These are the four lobes of the stomach; and on turning it over, you will see that the appendages which hang from the centre are arranged round the aperture which leads into the stomach.

Next examine the creature still more carefully, and you will find that a number of whitish lines radiate from the stomach to the circumference, some straight, while others are wavy and branched. In the Cyanea there are sixteen straight lines and as many branches. All these canals terminate in a wide vessel which runs round the edge of the disc. Here, then, is the digestive apparatus, showing a distinct advance on the animals of the sponge and coral, in which no such apparatus can be discovered.

Arranged round the edge of the disk are eight little brown spots, which are considered by Ehrenberg to be eyes, and indeed the Naked-eyed Jelly Fishes (*alias* the " Gymnophthalmic Medusiform Cœlenterata ") were formed into a distinct group. But I cannot accept these spots as eyes, and think that Ehrenberg was as hasty in considering them as such as he was in describing and figuring his so-called " Polygastric," *i.e.* many-stomached, "Infusoria." The many stomachs with their connecting tubes are plain enough in his figures, but no one except himself has succeeded in seeing them in the living objects. Professor Rymer Jones failed to find them, though he employed one of Ross's best microscopes, an instrument of far clearer definition than that used by Ehrenberg when writing his treatises; and even after inspecting the preparations made by that investigator he still retained his opinion.

Then other naturalists have credited the Medusæ with ears as well as eyes, asserting that certain organs situated at the base of the filaments surrounding the edge of the disc perform the function of ears. These organs are very small, scarcely exceeding the five-hundredth of an inch in diameter, and are irregular in number.

When examined with a microscope, each of these organs is seen to be a spherical sac or vesicle, containing

Fig 4.—RHIZOSTOMA.

from one to ten globular objects. Some observers say that these objects vibrate, while others have failed to detect the slightest movement. It has been conjectured, and in fact asserted, that the tiny objects within these vesicles are analogous to the ear-bones or "otoliths" of fishes, and so the sacs have been called "otolithic vesicles," and their function assumed to be connected with the sense of hearing. But I cannot accept these vesicles, irregular in number and variable in contents, as having any analogy to the ear structure of the higher animals, and am sure that their real office is yet to be discovered.

A few words about the development of the Medusæ must terminate this portion of the Jelly Fish's life-history.

The Medusa which we find lying on the sea-shore has not always possessed the same shape. It has not merely grown from a little Jelly Fish into a large one, any more than a house fly grows into a bluebottle, or a gnat into a daddy-longlegs.

It has passed through a series of changes before it has assumed the form in which we know it; but all individuals need not undergo the same changes. If we trace the creature through its previous existences, and suppose it to go through all of them, we first find it in the state of an egg. Thence issues an embryo covered with cilia, or hair fringes, by the movements of which it swims rapidly through the water. Then it settles down for its next change, affixes itself to a seaweed or similar object and becomes a bell-shaped animal, fixed by the base to the seaweed, and having long tentacles projecting from the edge of the bell. In this form it is a Hydra, like that of our fresh waters. Sometimes a slice splits off, as if cut with a knife, very much as do the offsets of a tulip bulb, and each slice becomes a separate Hydra capable of undergoing its own development, and thus escaping the two stages of egg and embryo.

The polyp continues to grow, and then certain little projections are seen upon various parts of the surface, just like the buds of plants. The buds increase rapidly, and become new polyps, throwing off secondary buds on their own account. The bud is technically termed a "gemma," to distinguish it from the offset, or "stolon."

When these gemmas have attained their full growth, a number of successive wrinkles surround the bell, and divide it into deep rings. In this stage it bears a curious resemblance to the grocer's salad-dressing bottles, where the quantity of glass is supposed to compensate for the paucity of its contents.

The next stage is that each ring becomes notched round the edge, so as to leave a number of projections. These projections increase in length until they become mere threads, while the divisions between the rings becomes deeper and deeper, so that each ring, or disk, as it has now become, is but slightly attached to its neighbours by the centre. Lastly, the central attachment gives way, the disks are set free, and each disk is then seen to be a small but perfect Medusa.

Such is a rapid and necessarily imperfect sketch of the varied processes through which a Medusa has to pass before it can assume the shape which we see lying on the seashore. We are apt to pass it without heeding it, and sometimes with even a feeling of disgust at its appearance; but its Maker has thought it of sufficient importance to cause it to pass through all these varied forms, each with its separate mode of organisation, before it can assume that shape which we mostly neglect and sometimes despise.

The second part of this history will treat of those Jelly Fishes which have no swimming disc, and do not come under the category of Medusæ.

SOME WONDERS OF THE SEA.

CHAPTER III.

JELLY FISHES—VARIETY AND BEAUTY.

AS a rule, the Jelly Fishes without pulsating discs are not to be found on the shore. For them we must go seawards and search for them in the waves.

Not that we shall be likely to see them, for in most of them the structure is too translucent to be distinguished from the water by any but the most practised eyes, and if the surface of the sea be in the least disturbed, they are absolutely invisible. Some, however, float upon the surface, and show some part of their structure above it.

Such, for example, is the creature called Porpita, in which the bell-shaped disc is modified into a flat, circular, gristly plate, which acts as a float, to which are suspended a vast number of tentacle-like appendages.

When closely examined, the float is found to be of very elaborate structure. Instead of being a simple cartilaginous disc as it appears at first sight to be, it is composed of a series of extremely thin circular plates, each succeeding one being larger than its predecessor. Each plate is scalloped round the edge, and marked with delicate lines, some radiating from the centre to the circumference, and others forming concentric circles, so as to produce a pattern very like the web of the garden spider.

The disc thus formed constitutes the skeleton—if we may employ such a word—of the animal, and it is clothed with a delicate membrane, falling into slight folds, nearly transparent, and of a lovely blue or purple colour. Surrounding the disc are the tentacles, which are set closely together and nearly cylindrical, though they enlarge slightly towards their tips.

As the disc does not pulsate, and the tentacles merely float in the water, the Porpita has no power of locomotion, and merely floats wherever the waves may happen to carry it. When thus displayed, it forms a most beautiful object. Lesson, in describing a species which he discovered (*Porpita Pacifica*) says that it resembles a small blue passion-flower as it floats on the water. Vast numbers of this creature are seen in company with each other, and Lesson saw the Porpitas in such fleets that they were closely pressed together, and covered the sea like a large sheet of ice.

Similarly possessed of a cartilaginous skeleton, the

Velella has a great advantage over the Porpita as far as locomotion goes. The disc is oval rather than circular, and across it there is an upright diagonal plate of the same material, which acts after the manner of a sail. The whole of the skeleton, including also the sail, is exceedingly thin, not thicker than tracing paper, but is wonderfully strong, considering its extreme tenuity. Like the disc of the Porpita, both sail and float are covered with radiating and concentric lines.

Sometimes, when southerly winds have been long prevalent, the Velella may be found on our coasts. I never had the fortune to see a living specimen, but a lady of my acquaintance once happened to be at Tenby when a large fleet of Velellas was driven on shore by the wind.

No inhabitant of Tenby appeared to have seen them before, but the sea-side people, with the inherent poetry of the Welsh language, immediately gave them the name of Sea Butterflies. My correspondent states that the gelatinous membrane which enveloped both sail and raft " was iridescent in a sort of vapoury transparent cloud of many tinted colours, blue and pale crimson predominating." With the letter a coloured sketch was sent, which exactly corroborated the verbal description.

She tried to keep the creatures alive, but utterly failed, as they all died within a very short time and began to putrefy, so that the only hope of preserving any portion lay in removing the membranes and drying the skeletons. This process was not a very easy one, for the dead Velellas putrefied so rapidly and exhaled so abominable an odour that, as their captor remarked, the Velellas and herself were simultaneously threatened with extermination. Two of them she kindly sent to me, and from them and the coloured drawing the above description is taken.

By sailors the Velella is called the Sallyman, this being the nautical equivalent for Sallee-man, the sail of the Velella bearing some resemblance to the lateen sail of the once-famous Sallee Rovers.

In the creature which now comes before us there is a sail, as in the Velella, but it is supported, not on a flat raft, but on a hollow float distended with air. Being rounded instead of flat, it would be upset by the slightest breeze were it not for the mass of tentacles and other appendages which hang deep in the water.

Popularly it is called by several names. "Portuguese man-of-war" is perhaps that by which it is best known, but sailors and other voyagers mostly persist in calling it by the name of Nautilus, and thereby puzzling their readers. I need scarcely say that so far from being one of the lowest forms of animal life, the Nautilus is one of the highest next to the vertebrates, that it has no sails, and that it either crawls on the bed of the sea, or projects itself through the water with its siphon-like tube, just as does the octopus, with which every one is now so familiar.

It has been well described as the most buoyant of animals. The depending tentacles are scarcely heavier than the water in which they are suspended, the distended float seems scarcely thicker than a soap bubble, and the only weight to be supported is that of the sail. Sometimes the float is eight or even nine inches in its longest diameter, and the appendages attain a length of several feet.

Like the Velella and Porpita, it has no power of directing its course, but is blown about by the wind at random, and is often found stranded on the shore. Now and then a continued southerly wind will bring it to our own coasts, but the occurrence is happily rare. The scientific name of Physalia is derived from a Greek word signifying a bladder, and the whole group of which it forms a part are called by the name of Physophoridæ, *i.e.* bladder-bearers.

Like the Porpita and Velella, the Physalia is a most lovely creature. Blue of various shades, deepening into purple on the crest or sail, is the usual hue of the portion that floats above the surface of the water, while the appendages that hang below from it are blue tinged with carmine. Both body and tentacles are of a crystalline translucency, so that a more beautiful object can hardly be imagined.

Attractive as it may be to the sense of sight, it is most offensive to that of touch, and no one who has once allowed a single filament to come in contact with his skin will do so a second time.

In the last chapter I described the weapons of the Stanger Jelly Fish. The Physalia is infinitely more formidable, and those who have experienced it both agree in saying that the Stanger is to the Physalia what a garden ant is to a hornet. These lovely trailing filaments are covered with myriads of poison sacs, so that the name of Portuguese man-of-war, which was given to them when the "Portugals" were the masters of the sea, was a singularly appropriate title.

The poison probably varies in its effects according to the constitution of the individual who is struck, but the strongest man is for a time reduced to helplessness.

Mr. Dutertre narrates his first encounter with a Physalia. He was alone in a little canoe, when he saw a Physalia floating on the sea. Not knowing what it was, he took hold of it for the purpose of examining it. No sooner had he touched it than the floating tendrils wound themselves on his hand and adhered as if glued to it.

The body of the animal was cool enough, but as soon as the filaments came upon his hand he felt as if the whole arm had been plunged into boiling water. Pang after pang shot through his frame, and though he was alone he could not refrain from shrieks for mercy, and cries that he was burning to death.

It is well known that the African slaves once employed in the West Indies brought with them the secrets of many poisons. These secrets were, however, only confided to a few of them, and these Obi men and women were equally feared by whites and those of their own colour. There is no doubt that Joanna, the beautiful and interesting girl who become the wife of Stedman, the celebrated traveller, died at the age of eighteen from Obi poison administered by a jealous rival.

For a long time it was thought that some of these poisons were procured from the Physalia, the sinuous tendrils being dried in the sun and reduced to powder. However, as the poison-sacs require their natural elasticity before they can act, it is evident that when they were dried they would lose all their potency. Accordingly, experiments were tried with the powder, and, as might have been anticipated, it was found to be perfectly harmless.

What may be the actual nature of the poison which produces such terrible effects is not, I believe, yet ascertained; and all we know is that it must be injected into the system before it can injure.

If it were possible to use a transparent surface and view the colours by transmitted light, as is done with the magic lantern, the artist might produce some approach to the singular beauty of the next group of Jelly Fishes, and the reader might partly appreciate it. As it is, the artist can only deal with black and white, and give a slight idea of the form, without attempting to render the colour, or even the graduating of light and shade.

So transparent are these beings, and so slightly different is their refractive power from that of the water in which they float, that even when enclosed in a glass vessel nothing is at first visible except water.

On examining the water more carefully, a little streak

of light is seen to gleam for a moment, and to vanish as suddenly as it appeared. Presently an opalescent spot shows itself and disappears. As the eye becomes more trained to take cognisance of these watery phantoms, they assume shape, and a certain amount of outline soon becomes visible. The many-coloured patches are then found to be the bodies of the imprisoned beings, and the streaks of light resolve themselves into threads as fine as those of a spider's web, floating in the water, and sometimes connecting a row of transparent globules strung together like pearls on a thread.

One of these inexpressibly beautiful creatures is indicated at Fig. 1. It is called in scientific language *Playa diphyes*, but I am not aware that it has any popular name. Indeed, like many other beautiful members of creation, it is so seldom seen that it could scarcely possess a popular name.

The word Diphyes is formed from the Greek, and signifies "double form." The name was given by Cuvier on account of the remarkable structure of the body, which looks like two distinct bodies slightly joined together. In later years, however, these double-bodied Jelly Fishes have been the objects of careful examination, and it is found that their swimming-cups or bells (*necto-calyces*) form part of a most complicated structure. They pulsate regularly, and with such force that the animals traverse the water with some rapidity, their long, slender filaments trailing after them much as the tail of a comet follows the head.

In consequence of possessing these swimming-cups, the whole group is distinguished by the name of Calycophoridæ, *i.e.* cup-bearers.

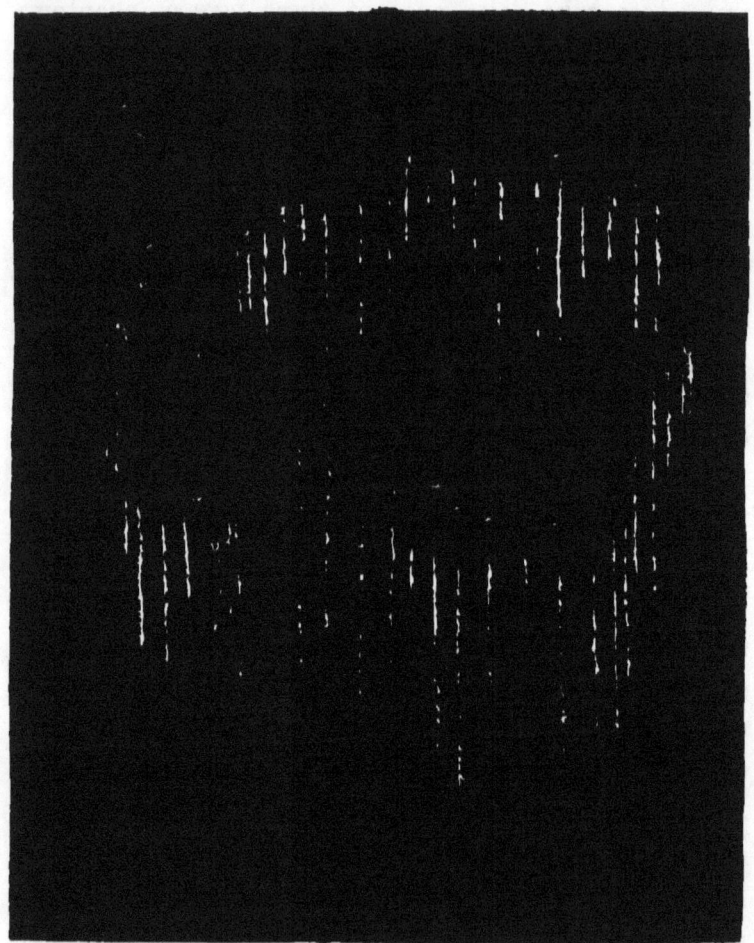

Fig. 1.—PLAYA DIPHYES.

To procure one of these creatures in a perfect state is an exceedingly difficult process.

Putting aside the fact that no one can distinguish them when in the sea, and that consequently bucketful after bucketful of water must be hauled up on the chance of finding a Diphyes in it, the extreme fragility of the threads offers a considerable obstacle to the searcher. They are even more easily broken than the spider's web, to which they have been compared, and the slightest touch will sever them from the double bell.

There is, however, just one hope. The trailing threads, although they can be shot out to a length of eighteen inches or more, can be almost entirely retracted into the body at the will of the animal. So, if the unaccustomed movement of the water caused by the bucket should induce the Diphyes to withdraw its threads, it may be safely transferred to the glass vessel which is waiting for it.

So delicate are those threads, that none of the Calycophores are found within many miles of land. Mid-Pacific is their usual home, and there they are tolerably plentiful. They can float unhurt in the long, rolling, smooth-topped billows, but the short, chopping seas caused by the beating of the waves against the shores, shatter to pieces such delicate organisms as theirs.

Although the double bells from which the Diphyes derives its name are most remarkable and complicated organisations, the chief interest of the creature lies in the system of "fishing-threads," as these delicate fibres are sometimes called.

In fact, the Calycophores seem in that respect very

like the long-armed fresh-water Polype, which has been for so many years a favourite object of investigation.

Although so small, the Hydra has the power of seizing the little animals which swim through the water. If they once come across a single tentacle of the Polype, their fate is certain. Their course is suddenly arrested, and although the thread be invisible to our eyes without the aid of a tolerably powerful magnifying-glass, the victim seems to be instantaneously paralyzed, and even if the first struggle on being seized should cause it to shake itself loose for a moment, it invariably dies.

It is worthy of remark that, in one of its many changes, the common Medusa assumes so precisely the form of the short-armed, fresh-water polype, that if the two animals were drawn to the same scale, and the portraits placed side by side, it would not be easy to say which was the perfect polype of the river, and which was the imperfect jelly fish of the sea.

A new arrangement of the various organs now comes before us: Fig. 2.

In the Diphyes, the principal thread, to which the pearl-like sacs and their pendent threads are attached, is very long. In the animals belonging to the Physophores it is quite short in proportion to the fishing-threads. The swimming bells are increased in number, and in this case there are six fully developed bells on each side. Below them are the tentacles and their appendages, and a torrent of fishing-threads hangs from them, looking like an inverted plume of spun glass. In one species, called

Fig. 2.—THE PHYSOPHORES.

Halistemma rubrum, there are at least sixty swimming bells, the chief stem being six or seven inches in length. The float is not more than a quarter of an inch long; the fishing-threads are about six or seven inches in length, and the mass of tentacles, capsules, and other organs is so great and so beautifully disposed, that the creature has been happily compared to a garland of transparent flowers endowed with life.

The details of construction which have been discovered in the Physophores are wonderfully beautiful, but our limited space will not allow of their description.

On our own coasts may be plentifully found several species of another group of thread-bearing jelly fishes. They move rapidly through the water, but by means of a paddle-like apparatus, and not by pulsating bells. On account of their shape they are popularly called Sea Acorns, and scientifically are known by the name of Cydippe or Beroë.

The species which is most commonly seen on our coasts is, when full grown, about as large as an ordinary acorn, and when taken out of the water looks just like a shapeless lump of translucent jelly. When placed in water it instantly vanishes, just as has been related of the previous species, and at first nothing can be seen of it except an occasional gleam of coloured light.

After a little while it becomes more distinctly visible, and then looks as if it were made of smooth glass, with slight bands traversing it from end to end, like the lines of longitude on a globe. Along these bands, and always in the same direction, little waves of opalescent light are seen to ripple, as beautiful and as changeable as the colours of a soap-bubble.

On account of the regularity of these colour-waves, the creatures were at one time called Fountain Fishes, the always changing hues being attributed to little streams of coloured liquid perpetually being ejected.

The creature is perpetually on the move, turning over and over, falling and rising, and proceeding in a series of graceful curves. Trailing from it there will soon appear two long, very slender filaments. These threads are of extreme delicacy, but on examining them a little more closely, each thread will be seen to have a row of filaments, comparatively short, but of still greater tenuity, attached to it throughout its whole length. These are the "fishing-threads," and the Cydippe will be seen to extend and contract the whole thread system at will, so that it is not of the same length for two consecutive seconds.

If several specimens be placed in the same vessel, they swim about quite freely, and it is a curious fact that although the trailing threads often come in contact with each other, they are never entangled, and in spite of their tenuity are not broken.

Through the transparent tissues the digestive organs are visible, but the most interesting portion of the structure is the mechanism by which the creature moves, and from which the rippling light-waves take their origin. With a little ingenuity it is always possible to bring the Cydippe close to the glass and keep it there, so that a microscope can be brought to bear on it. A half-inch power will be sufficient for most purposes.

If one of the longitudinal bands already mentioned be brought into focus, a most wonderful arrangement will be seen. The band is composed of a vast number of tiny flattened flaps, attached by one edge to the side of the animal, and, when at rest, overlapping each other like the tiles of a house. Supposing an ordinary Venetian blind to be only three inches long, but to retain the same width, it would present a good imitation of the structure. When the Cydippe moves, these little flaps rise and fall in rapid and regular succession, so that they act like the paddle floats of a steam-vessel. And, at the same time, their refractive power causes them to break up the light into its primary colours, and so to produce the beautiful opalescence which has been mentioned.

Even if the Cydippe be broken up by careless handling, the paddle-flaps will continue their rhythmical movements as long as they are not severed from their attachments, and so each piece swims about just as if it were a perfect animal.

The best way to capture these beautiful creatures without injuring them is to go out in a boat and tow a light net astern. I have always found that a common entomological net answers the purpose perfectly well. On a warm, calm day, the Cydippes float near the surface of the water, and can be taken in any number.

Suppose that we could take a Cydippe rather more than two inches in length, and roll it out as a cook rolls paste, until it forms a transparent ribbon some four or five feet in length, we should produce an object very much like the Venus' Girdle (*Cestum Veneris*).

The creature mostly inhabits the warmer seas, and is found on the shores of Naples, Nice, and other Mediterranean localities. The fishermen generally call it the Sea Sabre. When living and seen in the sunshine as it winds its graceful course through the transparent water, it is a wonderfully lovely creature, gleams of silvery radiance, melting into various shades of blue, pink, and purple, marking its shape.

At night it is perhaps even more strikingly beautiful, on account of the phosphorescence with which it is endowed, and resembles a ribbon of fire as it undulates through the water.

The digestive organs of the Cestum are seen traversing the centre of the body, and occupying a very small portion of the animal. There are several species of Cestum, but that which we have described is the most plentiful.

Not many years ago we knew comparatively nothing about the Jelly Fishes. Now we know just enough to indicate the treasures of knowledge which still lie hidden from us. I have, therefore, selected a few of the typical forms of the Jelly Fishes, hoping that the reader may be induced to study these wonderful creatures, and to see with his own eyes some of the living treasures of the deep.

I must, however, spare two or three lines to the wonderful fresh-water Medusa, discovered by Mr. W. Sowerby on June 10th, 1880. On that day he was looking into the warm-water tank of the Royal Botanic Society, when he saw a number of tiny Medusæ swimming in it. Up to that time Medusæ were thought to be exclusively marine, but here was a species inhabiting fresh water. Space is lacking for a full description of these wonderful little beings, and I can only say that some of them which were transferred to Kew multiplied rapidly, and I have seen them there swimming merrily about. The disc is about as large as a threepenny piece, and it pulsates about one hundred and twenty times in a minute. The scientific name of this little anomaly is *Limnocodium Sowerbii.*

SOME WONDERS OF THE SEA.

CHAPTER IV.

CORALS.

WHETHER dropping "like the gentle dew from heaven upon the earth beneath;" whether falling in tropical rain-torrents, and tearing its way seawards through solid rock; whether floating gently downwards in feathery snowflakes, or crashing all before it in the form of icy hail, the water which has been suspended in the atmosphere finds its way back to the sea, whence it was evoked by the sunbeams.

But it does not return unaccompanied, for the water that has rushed through many regions carries with it samples more or less discernible of the soils through which it has passed. Among others, an enormous amount of calcareous earth is continually poured into

SOME WONDERS OF THE SEA.

the sea by each river that reaches the final destination of its respective watershed.

What is to become of all this calcareous earth? If nothing were done with it, the sea would be so constantly receiving fresh supplies of solid matter, that the water would be gradually thickened, and daily become more like mud than water.

It cannot be destroyed, because destruction, as we understand the word, does not exist in nature. But it can be modified, and agencies may be imagined by which the calcareous matter is extracted from the water, and built up into fabrics which, though they differ in form from the chalky mud, are identical with it in material.

There are many such agencies, silently, slowly, but surely in constant work, and one of them I shall briefly describe in the following pages.

We know them, or rather the results of their labours, by the very comprehensive word CORAL, under which title are grouped a vast number of forms, all composed of calcareous matter, but differing greatly in the shapes which they assume and the structure of the living agencies which make them.

We have all heard of "Coral insects" and their work, and scarcely a generation ago the young learner was taught that the Coral Insect was the founder of tropical islands, having raised its edifices from the depths of the ocean, and only being checked in its labours when it reached high-water mark. There is a certain amount of truth in this statement, but more than an equal amount of error is mixed with it. In the first place it is scarcely necessary to mention that the coral-formers are not insects, but creatures of an infinitely lower organisation; and, in the next place, they can only live within a very limited distance of the surface of the water.

Putting aside the systematic division of these wonderful creatures and their productions, we will consider them all as Corals, whether they be true Corals, Madrephylles, Gorgonias, Tubipores, Alcyonidæ, &c., &c., and trace, as far as possible, the course of their lives, and the nature of their horny or stony skeletons.

Some of these beings are much more simple in structure than the others, and we will therefore begin with them.

Supposing that we take a rather coarse sponge, especially if it has been in use for some time, and compare it with the common Mushroom Madrepore, we must at once see that there is a marked analogy between them, even though we are only looking at the dead skeleton.

In fact, if we could take a common sponge, and transmute it into stone instead of silex, we should have an object so exactly like a madrepore that it would be very difficult to distinguish the one from the other.

If we were able to procure their living investments, we should see an analogy and a resemblance between them, but not an identity.

The Sponge Animal belongs to the great group of

Protozoa, the very lowest form in which animal life can definitely be said to exist. But the Coral animal belongs to a more highly organised group, the simplest of which

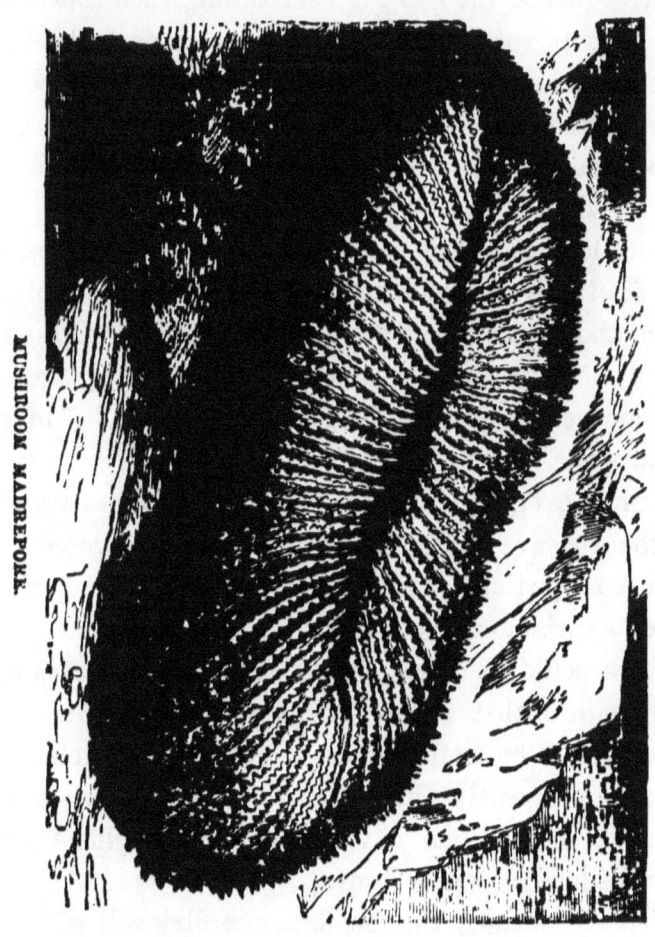

MUSHROOM MADREPORE.

is called Madrephylle, and the most complex are popularly known as Sea Anemones.

Scientifically they are called "Anthozoa," *i.e.* Living-

Flowers, because in many of the species the tentacles have so floral an aspect, that for many centuries they were considered to be flowers of the sea, having, like the sensitive plants, the habit of contracting when touched.

It is only with those Anthozoa which deposit a solid skeleton that we have at present to deal, and so we will proceed at once to the Madrephylles, the best-known example of which is that which has been already mentioned.

If we look at the upper surface of the Madrepore, we shall see that it presents a curiously striking resemblance to the under surface of the common mushroom, a number of thin laminæ, or stony plates, radiating from a common centre, just as do the vegetable "gills" of the mushroom.

Turn it over, and a number of rounded ridges are seen on the concave under-surface, each being covered with thorny projections, and having between each pair of ridges a variable number of the small thin laminæ.

If we could re-invest this mass of stony plates with the creature that formed them, we should find that there would be nothing but a thin film of gelatinous matter, apparently without any more appearance of a living structure than if it were so much glue washed over the laminæ with a brush.

Yet, if touched, the membranous film will withdraw itself between the laminæ, and not return to its place until some time after the irritating cause has been removed.

Organs it has none—at least, none that have as yet been detected. There seem to be no tentacles for inducing currents of water to pass over its surface, no mouths for the admission of food, no digestive organs, no nerves, and no muscles.

Still, in some way to us unknown, this shapeless and apparently inorganic film is able to assume a definite form, to separate from the sea-water the calcareous particles which are floating in it, and to build them up into the beautifully elaborate arrangement of hard, stony plates which is shown in the figure as well as the art of the draughtsman and engraver can transfer it to paper. It is prepared in—

> "the unknown abyss
> "Of Nature's laboratory, where she hides
> Her deeds from every eye except her Maker's."

It might seem that when once the stony particles were deposited and arranged, they must be out of the control of the creature that separated them from the sea-water. But careful investigations have shown that the earthy matter is deposited in the substance of the film, and that its particles can not only be deposited by the animal, but removed as occasion requires, or even absorbed again into the gelatinous film. There are vast numbers of these fungus-like Madrephylles, another well-known example of which is the common Brain-stone Coral, *Mæandrina*, so called because its convolutions and general shape present a striking resemblance to the human brain when removed from the skull.

K

Many of the common Madrepores look very much as if a vast number of the Mushroom Madrephylles had been moulded into a convex mass, very much diminished in size, and viewed through the pseudoscope, so that each individual appears concave instead of convex.'

Those, however, which are the most conspicuously apparent in their submarine office are the beautiful species which are here represented by the Plantain Madrepore (*Madrepora plantaginea*), so common in drawing-room ornaments. These are the formers of the so-called Coral Islands, and in spite of the small size of the living polypes, and the minuteness of the calcareous particles which they deposit, they actually alter the surface of the globe so rapidly that important changes are made within the compass of a single human lifetime, and the physical geography of enormous tracts is entirely transformed.

In the first place, it must be understood that not even the apparently inorganic film of the Madrephylles can exist at any great depth of water, a certain amount of light and warmth being necessary for them. When we come to the better organised beings which produce the true Madrepores, we find that a larger supply of light and warmth is required, and that in consequence they are brought more within the scope of personal observation. Moreover, the water is so translucent in such localities that objects are clearly discernible at a depth of forty or fifty feet.

The whole surface of the Madrepore is covered with

polypes of various sizes and colours, furnished with feathery arms that radiate like the petals of a flower, and are perpetually in motion, evidently for the sake of

PLANTAIN MADREPORE.

catching food. If touched, the polype contracts itself into the soft, gelatinous film from which it had proceeded, and is only visible as a small and slightly projecting tubercle. The spot on which each polype has rested is marked in the stony skeleton by being the centre to which all the little laminæ converge.

If these polype-cells be examined with a tolerably powerful lens, a wonderful beauty of structure will be revealed, the little spicules of which the general mass is composed being arranged with a regularity that wonderfully resembles the ice-crystals of the snowflake.

Care must be taken to hold it in a good light; the system on which the structure is based will then be easily seen.

Round the edge of the aperture are ranged in order a vast number of the white stony spicules of which the mass is composed.

Radiating from the circumference towards the centre, but not quite meeting, are six very delicate laminæ. When viewed directly from above, so that only their upper edges are seen, they look very like the spokes of a wheel, and indeed have been so represented in more than one book, the artist having evidently drawn from a microscopical preparation. If, however, we take a piece of the Madrepore in our hands, and turn it about as we are examining it with the lens, we shall find no difficulty in tracing the laminæ down to the extremity of the cell, if we may so call it.

As each of these cells was once inhabited by a living six-armed polype, always keeping its beautiful tentacles in motion, it is easy to imagine the extreme beauty of the object when its living envelope is still encrusting it.

How the Coral Islands are produced must now be seen.

The bed of the ocean is not one uniform plain, but, like the surface of the earth, has its deep valleys and lofty mountains. Sometimes, the tops of the mountains are not covered by water, and then we call them islands; but they are not the Coral Islands of which we are now treating.

These appear mysteriously, and give no premonitions of their appearance. A ship, perhaps, passes over the track which has been traced by hundreds of vessels previously, strikes upon a rock that is not in the charts, and sinks. She has come upon a coral island that has not yet reached the surface, but which in a few years will be known, and its place noted in the charts.

Below the surface is the apex of a mountain-peak, submerged so deeply that a ship cannot touch it with her keel. But upon that peak the Coral colonies have settled, and have continued their hidden work until their sharp, stony ridges have gradually approached the surface, and become a danger to the next vessel that sails in that direction.

By degrees, the Coral reaches the limits of high water, and the polypes which make it not being able to exist without water, can rise no higher, but spread laterally in all directions, until, according to Captain Basil Hall's graphic simile, it looks like a huge cauliflower on its stem. Consequently, there is deep water within a foot of its edge, the lead gives no warning, and so a vessel is wrecked without any fault of those in charge of her.

Another well-known form of Coral Island is that which forms a large circle. There is deep water close to the edge both inside and outside, forming a natural harbour so perfect that although a tempest may rage outside it, there is smooth water within. This is also due to a submarine mountain.

In those regions volcanic action is a conspicuous element, and volcanoes, both active and extinct, are plentiful. When an extinct volcano rears its summit tolerably near the surface of the sea, the Coral-makers are sure to settle upon it sooner or later. As the Coral must necessarily be founded on the edge of the crater, it is evident that when it reaches the surface of the water it must retain the circular form. The Coral, not being able to extend itself upwards, in consequence being almost invisible by day, and quite so at night, both these types of Coral Islands would become exceedingly dangerous, and, indeed, make navigation almost impossible. But another provision steps in, and not only robs them of their terrors, but converts them into havens of rest and safety.

Before very long, seaweeds accumulate, and are flung by the storms upon the surface of the "reef," as the Coral mass is called. Mixed with the seaweed are quantities of marine worms, molluscs, and other specimens of ocean life. Being unable to exist out of the water, they die, and by their decay form a fertile earth capable of affording nourishment to plants of a higher order.

Floating cocoa-nuts, which have the power of drifting

for immense distances while retaining the principle of life, are arrested by the new reef, strike root, and become the progenitors of palm-trees innumerable. Birds are sure to follow, bringing with them the seeds of various plants, and so by degrees the almost invisible coral-reef becomes a fertile island.

Man then visits the newly-formed region, attracted by the waving palm-trees, and finds a spot exactly suited to his wants. The natives of these climates are essentially maritime, and nothing better for them could be imagined than this palm-fringed ring of fertile land resting upon its coral base. In its centre is an absolutely perfect harbour, affording refuge for their canoes in stormy weather. The harbour is, in fact, the crater of the submerged volcano, so that whether within or without, the vessels can be brought so close to the shore that the tops of the cocoa-palms actually overhang the masts of the canoes.

Food is to be found in abundance. As to vegetable food, there are, in the first place, the cocoa-nut palms, each of which trees can afford subsistence to a family. Then there are sure to be bread-fruits, yams, pine-apples, mangoes, and the other vegetable productions which thrive so abundantly in tropical regions.

Animal food is found in abundance in the sea. Fishes come for shelter in the coral-reefs, and absolutely swarm under the overhanging ledges of rock. The interior of the island is also full of them, the central lake with its quiet waters being precisely what the fishes most need, and becoming a vast natural fish-hatching establishment.

Cuttles, which are largely eaten by the natives, also hide in the rocky crevices, and are deluded to their destruction by cunningly devised baits made of cowrie-shells. The turtles also abound in these seas, and when the time comes for depositing their eggs, haunt the shore in search of convenient nurseries.

So, by the unseen and unheard labours of the Coral-makers, the earthy particles which were entangled in the water are separated and built into a form suitable for the habitation of Man, thus giving him more earth to replenish and subdue, and enabling him to fulfil more completely the mission for which he was created.

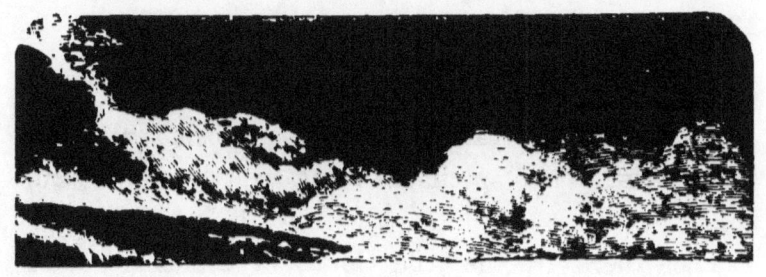

SOME WONDERS OF THE SEA.

CHAPTER V.

CORALS—FORM AND ACHIEVEMENTS.

HAVING now glanced at the most conspicuous achievements of the Corals, we will take a hasty review of some of the endlessly varied forms which they assume.

There are the various Caryophylle Madrepores, specimens of which are favourite inhabitants of marine aquaria, the lovely colours of their animal envelope being even more attractive to the eye than the delicate stony laminæ which they deposit. Several species are found on our own southern coasts. The Goblet Caryophylle, which is here given of its natural size, is a good type of this group. The reader must imagine to himself that the groundwork of this beautiful object is pure dead white, and that the upper portion is coloured with crimson, yellow, "cau-de-Nile" green, pale grey, and other hues, no two specimens being exactly of the same colour.

Then there are the true Corals of commerce, sometimes white, sometimes red, and sometimes pink, the

GOBLET CARYOPHYLLE.

last-mentioned being of the most value in the manufacture of ornaments.

All the true Corals have the stony core solid and branch-like, and slightly grooved on the exterior. At irregular intervals there are small rounded projections, radiated in star-like fashion above. These mark the spots in which the living polypes were placed, the remainder being covered with the common gelatinous envelope to which they are attached, or rather from which they proceed. If a transverse section be made of a branch of Coral, it will be seen to have some resemblance to the porcupine quill, or the spine of the sea-urchin, the lines of the corrugated surface being continued inwards until they nearly meet in the centre.

A SECTION OF CORAL.

The preceding illustration shows the transverse section as it appears when ground down and polished, so as to be placed under the microscope.

The ordinary appearance of the polypes, when extended and withdrawn, is shown in the illustration on next page.

One of them is represented as fully extended, and standing out boldly from the general mass, its eight fringed tentacles fully extended for the capture of food.

Just on its right is a half-extended polype, and below is one which is just beginning to protrude its arms. The rounded projections with their star-like radiations show the position of other polypes which have withdrawn themselves into the general envelope.

As in the common red Coral the general envelope is

CORAL POLYPES.

scarlet, and the polypes are snowy white, the extreme beauty of the living creature can be easily imagined.

The whole life-history of the Coral is singularly interesting, dating from the day when it swims freely through the water in search of a favourable locality, to the time when it has settled down and developed into the beautiful branched structure with which we are so familiar.

In the true Corals the branches are short, stout, and

sturdy, and therefore capable of sustaining the force of the waves. But there are some allied species which have very long and slender branches, which would be broken to pieces by a wave which has no effect on the true Coral. On account of the tangled mode in which the branches of these beings are interlaced, they are called Gorgonias by the scientific. Fishermen mostly know them by the name of Sea Fans, or Fan Corals, because they are flat and spread in fan-fashion from the base. In some of them the animal envelope is a bright scarlet, and retains its colour after it is dry, so that a good specimen of Gorgonia is really a handsome object.

The spicules which are deposited by the animal are wonderful objects when seen under a moderate microscopical power, say a half-inch object-glass. They are transparent, stick-shaped, covered with knobs, and having the most lovely tints of pink, very pale blue, and yellow. Indeed, they look so much like barley-sugar that all young people to whom I have shown the spicules through the microscope have said that they *must* be good to eat, if they were only large enough.

In all these curious beings the central axis of the stem and branches is composed alternately of horny matter and stone, the former producing flexibility, and the latter giving strength. When beaten by the waves this compound structure yields to their force, and is enabled to recover itself again when the force of the storm has passed away.

Another beautiful and well-known example of this group is the Organ-pipe Coral, of which there are several kinds. That which is best known is figured in the accompanying illustration, Fig. 2 being a portion drawn of its natural size. The colour of the tubes is pinky red, and as the animal that deposits it is bright green, the appearance of a living specimen is singularly beautiful.

These tubes radiate slightly from each other, though they can scarcely be said to have a common centre. They are supported at intervals by horizontal laminæ, through which they pass, so that they bear a resem-

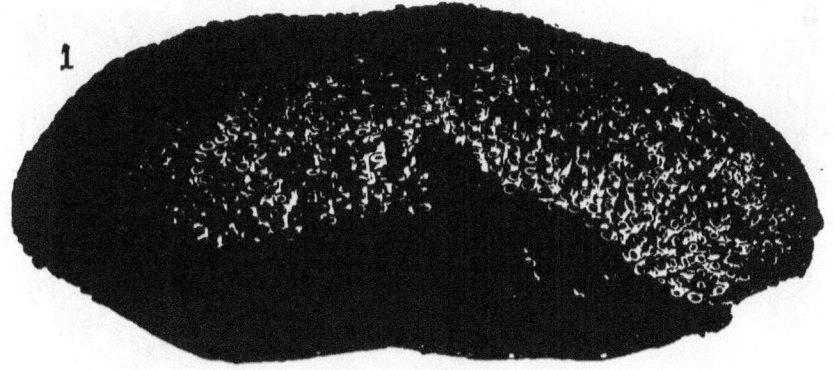

ORGAN-PIPE CORAL.

blance to the arrangement of organ pipes too evident to be unnoticed.

Now and then they envelop a stone, shell, or other foreign object, and in such cases have a curious way of turning aside for a space, and resuming their original course when they have passed round the obstruction. An example of such a modification is seen on the left side of Fig. 2.

In all the species belonging to this group, the polypes,

instead of being on the outside of the stony deposit, are within it, forming it into tubes, in and out of which they can freely project the tentacle by which they obtain food.

At Fig. 1 is seen a mass of Organ-pipe Coral, considerably reduced, so as to show its general appearance. At Fig. 2 a portion is given of the natural size, so as to show the arrangement of the tubes. Fig. 3 represents two of

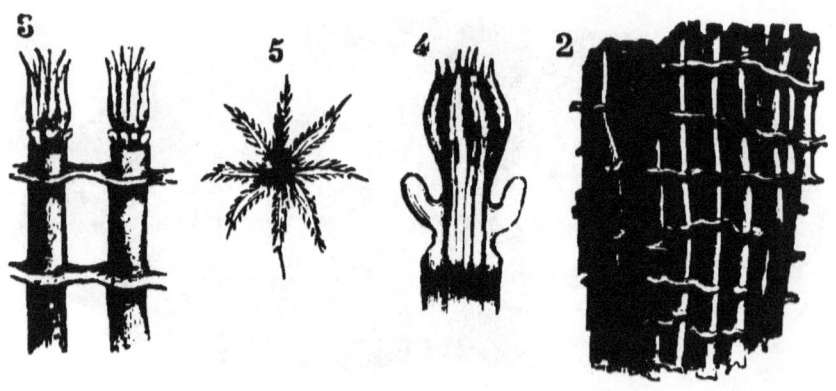

ORGAN-PIPE CORAL.

the tubes enlarged, showing the "head," as the tentacle mass is called, as it appears when it is just protruded, and enabling the reader to understand the mode in which the tentacles are pressed together when within the tube. Fig. 4 gives a further magnified view of a single head, and Fig. 5 shows the appearance of a single individual when fully expanded, seen from above, and considerably magnified.

These beings enter largely into the constituents of

Coral Islands, and occur most numerously within the tropics. They are, however, found in most of the warmer seas, either north or south of the equator, and are very plentiful in the Red Sea.

How these tubes and their supporting laminæ are produced no one as yet knows. It seems that there *must* be vessels or secreting sacs, but none have as yet been found. How the creature is able to protrude and retract itself, spread or fold its tentacles, is another mystery. There are no perceptible muscular fibres, still less any nerves, by which the will of the animal—for it evidently has a will—can be conveyed to them. We do know that the membrane is capable of contraction and relaxation, but there our knowledge ceases.

The last of these wonderful beings that can be mentioned is the Sea Pen.

These remarkable compound animals are not attached to any object which could support them, but seem to lie loosely at the mercy of the waves. They are all more or less phosphorescent, and at night have a peculiarly striking appearance, owing to their graceful and boldly curved outlines. The Sea Pens are to be found in nearly all the warmer seas, and are common in the Mediterranean.

THE MOST GIFTED INSECT RACE.

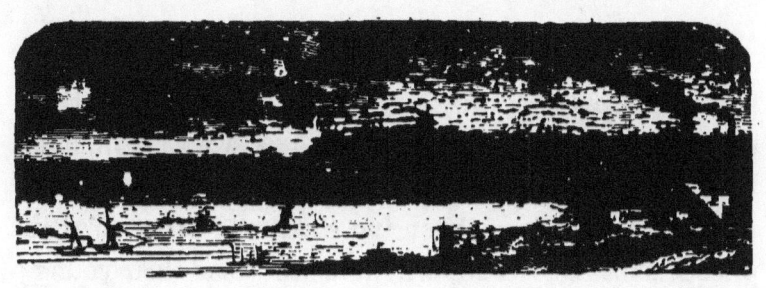

THE MOST GIFTED INSECT RACE.

CHAPTER I.

ANT LIFE.

WITHOUT brains, dull in colour, and insignificant in size, the Ants are not only the most wonderful of the insect race, but, next to man, perhaps the most gifted of the whole animal kingdom. Sir J. Lubbock, who has made a special study of these insects, goes so far as to say that although the anthropoid apes approach more nearly to man in bodily structure than any other animals, the "Ants have a fair claim to rank next to man in the scale of intelligence."

Yet, though they have no brain, but only a series of nervous ganglia connected by threads, they possess reasoning powers and are marvellously intelligent; can work in concert under leaders; can converse with each other; possess enduring memories; evince love, hatred, and compassion; can play as well as work; will fight with desperate courage in defence of their homes; will make war against neighbouring states and carry off their prisoners into servitude; will nurse and tend their young; will keep milch cattle in sheds built expressly for them; will lay up stores of honey and grain; will till the soil, weed the ground, plant seeds, and reap the harvest; and lastly, when their brief life is over, even bury their honoured dead with elaborate ceremony.

How the little creatures can perform these tasks, some of them being beyond the capacity of many a savage tribe, and yet possess no brains, is one of the many seeming paradoxes with which the study of animal life teems.

It is obvious that with insects possessing such a life-history, even a tolerably full account would occupy several large volumes. I shall therefore content myself with giving a slight sketch of Ant Life, illustrating as many as possible of the characteristics which have been mentioned.

As to locality, the ants are distributed over all the warmer portions of the Globe. Cold they cannot endure, though some of them, which inhabit tropical countries, can run about at ease on ground so heated by the tropical sunbeams, that a slice of raw meat would soon be cooked if laid upon it.

In fact, the ant tribes are dispersed round the earth in a broad belt, thickest at the equator, and thinning off gradually towards the poles. The wonderful heat-enduring power of the ants has been admirably described by Dr. Livingstone.

"In the midst of this dreary drought it was wonderful to see those tiny creatures, the ants, running about with their accustomed vivacity. I put the bulb of a thermometer *three inches under the soil* in the sun, at midday, and found the mercury to stand at 132° to 134°.

"If certain kinds of beetles were placed on the surface, they ran about for a few seconds and expired. But this broiling heat only augmented the activity of the long-legged black ants; and not only were they, in this sultry weather, able individually to moisten soil to the consistency of mortar, but when the inner chambers of their galleries was laid open, they were surprisingly humid. Yet there was no dew, and the house being placed on a rock, they could have no subterranean passage to the bed of the river, which ran about three hundred yards below the hill.

"Can it be that they have the power of combining the oxygen and hydrogen of their vegetable food, by vital force, so as to form water?"

To begin with their place in the scale of nature.

Ants belong to the Hymenoptera, in common with bees, wasps, ichneumons, and sun-flies. Like many of the bees and wasps, they are social in their habits, but they differ from these insects in many respects.

In common with the social bees and wasps, they are divided into males, females, and workers. But the workers of the bees and wasps possess wings, whereas in the ants these organs are restricted to the males and females, and are only borne by them for a short time. Then, the front wings of the wasps can be folded longitudinally when the insect is at rest, while those of the ants remain as permanently spread as those of a butterfly.

In order to gain a general idea of Ant Life, we cannot do better than examine a nest of our most common

ANTS.

British species, the Garden Ant (*Formica nigra*). This is sometimes, but erroneously, called the Black Ant; that name properly belonging to another species (*Formica fuliginosa*), sometimes called the Jet Ant. This latter insect is a dull, sluggish creature, not appearing in the open air more than it can help, and entirely distinct from the active, fussy Garden Ant.

Any one who has kept a garden must be familiar with

this insect, which is apt to be very annoying, in consequence of its fondness for ripe fruit.

Sometimes its numbers are incalculable. The late Mr. F. Smith writes of it as follows: "In the month of September, 1855, I observed at Dover immense clouds of this ant passing over the town towards the sea. Subsequently, on passing along the beach, I observed a line of their floating bodies extending from the town at least a mile towards St. Margaret's. The line consisted of males and females, and was nearly a yard wide."

There is never any difficulty in finding an ant's nest, as there is always a stream of workers passing in and out of the dwelling, and keeping so regularly to one track that they make a beaten path easily traceable even when no ants are on it. These paths invariably end in a hole in the ground—mostly at the edges of gravel paths in gardens—and the holes can be distinguished from those made by worms by the little pellets of earth brought out of the furrows and heaped near the entrance.

The end of summer is the best time for examining the nests. On opening one of them a marvellously busy scene is disclosed. Ants are running about in all directions, and most of them are carrying in their jaws the whitish oval objects which at one time were thought to be grains of corn, but which are now popularly called "ants' eggs." Bird-dealers make great use of them in feeding certain birds, especially the nightingale.

In this country ants do not store food in their nest; and even if they did, they are mostly carnivorous in their habits, and could not eat corn. Neither are these objects eggs, and indeed, a moment's thought would show that the ant could not be the parent of an egg larger than itself. Very few persons have ever seen an ant's egg, or would recognise it if they did.

The eggs are exceedingly minute, of a very pale yellow, and kept carefully out of danger. When they are hatched they produce tiny grubs, very much like those of the bee or wasp, and quite as helpless. These little grubs are watched and fed by the worker ants, being quite incapable of procuring food for themselves. When these grubs are full fed they envelop themselves in a cocoon, which they spin just as does the caterpillar of the silkworm. These cocoons are the so-called "ants' eggs," and, if they be examined with a magnifying-glass, the silken threads of which they are composed can be easily traced. In fact, they look just like the cocoons of the silkworm after the loose silk has been wound off (page 157).

They can be cut open with a pair of fine scissors, and then, according to the time of year, there will be found within them either the footless grub, the pupa, or the perfect insect. It will be noticed that the cocoons are of three sizes. The largest are those of the wing-bearing females, the next largest those of the wing-bearing males, and the smallest those of the wingless workers.

The chief object of the ceaseless labour for which the ant is proverbial, is the nurture of the helpless grub and the care of the equally helpless pupa.

Scattered about the nest may be seen the perfect

insects, conspicuous by their wings and large proportionate size. They are curiously helpless, and seem quite bewildered at being exposed to the light. All they can do is to crawl slowly under cover, but, unless they are led by the workers, they seem incapable even of discovering the open passages leading to the interior of the nest.

Suddenly, urged by an irrepressible instinct, the winged ants of both sexes issue from the nest and take to the air. They have but small powers of flight, and can make no way against a breeze, with which they drift as helplessly as do the locusts.

Sometimes, as in the case recorded by Mr. Smith, their numbers are incalculably large, and if all that rise from the earth were to descend in safety and found new colonies, the ants would soon render the country uninhabitable by man.

But, just as in the great yellow pollen clouds which may be seen drifting from the Scotch fir, only a comparatively few grains are needed for their important office, so out of these ant clouds only a very few pairs survive. They are eaten in vast quantities by birds, but the greater number are driven by the wind into the water, and there perish.

The object of their flight is the same as with the queen bees, *i.e.* to meet their mates in the air; and even on the most favourable days, when there is warm sunshine and little or no wind, the flight is but a short one.

Those that descend in safety run about for a minute

or two, and then go through the curious process of depriving themselves of their wings. They do not bite them off, as has often been stated—at least in any case which I have seen—but force the wings forward, press the tips against the ground, and with a sharp jerk snap them off close to the body.

The wings are not torn out from their sockets, and there are no marks on them as of teeth. They are

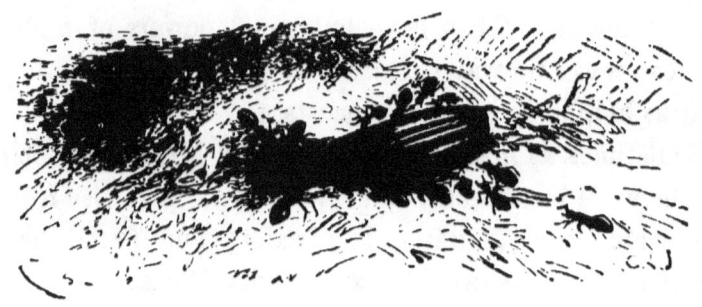

ANTS DRAGGING BEETLE.

simply snapped asunder, and, after the operation is concluded, the short stumps of the four wings can be seen projecting from the thorax.

It is easy to distinguish the males from the females, although they both possess wings. The males are but little larger than the workers, while the females are twice as large, and hardly look as if they belonged to the same species.

How a new colony is founded is as yet unknown. That a queen from an existing community will not be received by other subjects has been conclusively proved

ANTS AND THEIR TINY GRUBS

by Sir John Lubbock. He several times took a queen of the common Yellow Ant and placed her among a number of her own species. They not only refused to recognise her as a queen, but attacked and killed her.

Probably, on her return to earth, the young queen rejoins the nest, assembles a number of workers, and with their help founds the new colony. At all events, it seems to have been proved that without the assistance of workers young larvæ cannot be nourished.

However this may be, new colonies are formed, and increase with astonishing rapidity, the inmates of a single nest being reckoned by the thousand.

In such an assemblage as this it is evident that there must be some definite organisation. Even in our common English ants this organising power is manifest, while in many exotic species the discipline is as exact and severe as that of an European army.

In the first place a strange ant, even of the same species, is never admitted to a nest. Larvæ and pupæ will be received and bred up as members of the community, but perfect insects, whether males, females, or workers, would be attacked and probably killed.

Now, how do the ants detect a stranger ?

It is not likely that all the individual ants of a hundred thousand members of a nest should be mutually known.

Neither do they communicate by some pass-word, as has been suggested. For when larvæ and pupæ were taken out of one nest and hatched in another, they were acknowledged as friends when restored to the nest whence they had been taken. Had any form of language been used, it would have been that of the nest where it was hatched and nurtured, just as an English baby, if reared by French people, would speak French and not English when it grew to man's estate.

Yet, language of some sort the ants certainly have, or their leaders could not give commands or the subordinates obey them. Their powers of united action are really wonderful.

I have repeatedly placed dead insects near the nest of the common Wood Ant, for the sake of watching their powers of combination. As soon as the prey is discovered, messengers convey the tidings into the interior of the nest, and in a short time the dead insect is surrounded by the ants, which seem to come from all directions at once. They immediately set to work at their task, some pushing and some pulling, but all acting on a concerted plan, until they contrive to drag it up the steep side of their dwelling. Should it be a large insect, as is represented in the illustration, they leave it at one of the entrances, and do not reappear for some time. What they do during this interval I do not know, but fancy that they must be engaged in making arrangements for its reception. Sooner or later, however, they again resume the labour, push and pull the insect out of sight, and then proceed to repair the entrance through which it has been dragged, and which has been too much enlarged by the passage of its body (page 156). From the concerted mode of action employed in such cases, it is evident that some mode of speech must be used for the conveyance of ideas. But what the language may be is not easy even to conjecture.

When two ants meet, they usually touch each other's antennæ, and evidently communicate ideas to each other. This practice, however, does not account for the perfect military discipline which prevails in the community, and the mode in which the leaders convey their ideas to large bodies of subordinates.

Touching antennæ would be a very slow process, and there is evidently some analogue of our bugle call, which all can understand and obey simultaneously. What it is we do not know. It may be possible that it consists of sounds too acute to be detected by human ears. And yet, although the microphone makes the step of the ant's feet as audible as the tread of a horse, nothing approaching to a vocal sound has as yet been detected.

For two purposes this power of communication is necessary—*i.e.* for war or foraging, or perhaps both, as we shall soon see.

THE MOST GIFTED INSECT RACE.

CHAPTER II.

THEIR MODE OF FIGHTING.

THE mode of fighting among ants differs according to the species, but in most cases they direct their attacks against the antennæ of the adversary.

Here is an account of an ant-fight which occurred lately. It was sent to me by a schoolmaster friend, whose duties unfortunately prevented him from seeing the completion of the battle.

"I saw a grand fight on Friday last between one small black ant (evidently the Garden Ant, *Formica nigra*) and three big wood ants. One wood ant had got poor blackie tight round the waist. Wood ant No. 2 had been fooling around blackie's jaws with its antennæ.

Blackie promptly availed himself of one, and held on. There was a great whirligig going on.

"Enter wood ant No. 3, investigates matter and makes a great onslaught on poor blackie, who, however, will not let go. After a while No. 3, not being himself troubled as to his antennæ, discovers that he has business elsewhere, and goes. Same struggle goes on for another ten minutes. No man could have held out for five.

"At last I detach No. 1, who goes off in dudgeon. Blackie and No. 2 have a grand rough-and-tumble, or rather, several rough-and-tumbles, but they all end with the same *status quo*. Blackie still holds on like grim death, and No. 2 continues backing and dragging blackie up hill and down dale for more than twenty minutes. Then the school-bell rang, and I had to go, leaving them fighting. I wonder what became of blackie."

The tenacity with which ants will retain their hold far exceeds that of the bulldog. Like that animal, they will allow themselves to be killed sooner than loosen their hold; but unlike the dog, the jaws do not relax their grip after death. It is quite common to see one ant encumbered by the head of a dead foe hanging on its legs by the jaws; and with some exotic species, the only plan when attacked is, to pull the bodies away from the heads, and detach the jaws afterwards.

During a recent visit to Plymouth, I witnessed a curious example of this tenacity.

Mr. G. C. Bignell, a gentleman well known in the

entomological world, was showing me his collection of insects. Among the ants was a singular group, so "mixed" that its component parts could not be easily discriminated without the aid of a magnifying-glass.

The group was then seen to consist of two ants, a worker Wood Ant, and a winged male of a smaller species (*Myrmica scabrinodes*), much resembling the common Garden Ant. The former had seized the latter, and was carrying it off to its own nest, when its progress was interrupted by capture. Although itself a prisoner, it did not loosen its hold, and even after both insects had been killed by chloroform, it retained its grasp.

Not only do the jaws of some ants retain their grip after death, but they continue to bite. They have a kind of sawing movement, each jaw forcing itself alternately into the wound, and causing quite as much pain as if the creature were alive. In some parts of Brazil, the natives make use of certain sickle-jawed ants as extemporised sutures for wounds. They simply pinch the edges of the wound together, and hold the ant to it. The creature immediately bites at the obstacle, making its jaws meet. The native surgeon pulls away the body, leaving the head still adhering, and so proceeds until the wound is firmly sewn together by the ants' jaws. Seven or eight ant-heads are sometimes employed for a single wound.

Isolated combats do frequently take place, as in the instance already recorded, and of such combats the spectators take very little notice. But when a warlike expedition is undertaken, each ant has its own place and own work, and will fight to the death in obeying orders. The Wood Ant seldom fights singly, issuing from the nest in solid battalions, while the Red Ant will fight individually or in concert with equal alacrity. Each species seems to have its own method of fighting.

One species, *Formica exsecta*, is, according to Sir J. Lubbock, a very remarkable insect, attacking its larger foes much as the billmen of olden days attacked knights in full armour.

"It is a delicate, not to say active species. They advance in serried masses, but at close quarters they bite right and left, dancing about to prevent being bitten themselves. When fighting with larger species, they spring on to their backs and seize them by the neck or by one antennæ.

"They also have the instinct of combining in small parties, three or four seizing one enemy at once, and then pulling different ways, so that she, on her part, cannot get at any one of her foes. One of them then jumps on her back, and cuts, or rather saws, off her head. In battles between this ant and the much larger *Formica pratensis*, many of the latter may be seen, each with a little *F. exsecta* on her back, sawing off her head from behind."

So redoubtable a fighter is this little ant, that an instance was known where a single nest had established at least two hundred colonies, and throughout a circle of about four hundred yards in diameter, had extirpated almost every other ant, only one species remaining to defy it by means of superior agility. M. Forel, who describes this enormous nest, calculates that its inhabitants numbered half a million.

The reader will notice that the feminine pronoun is used in this account. Male ants never fight, nor do the perfect females. All fighting devolves upon the imperfect females, or Amazons, as they are sometimes called. As we shall presently see, there are some species of ant in which the undeveloped females are divided into two great bodies, one being intended for working and being comparatively small, and the other intended for fighting, and not only of very great comparative size, but furnished with large and powerful jaws.

Plunder and slave-catching are the chief objects of these expeditions. In our own country the species most celebrated for its slave-hunting proclivities is the Red Ant (*Formica sanguinea*). This creature is mostly to be found in the southern parts of England, and especially haunts the New Forest, where it loves to makes its nest in banks of dry soil

THE MOST GIFTED INSECT RACE.

CHAPTER III.

PLUNDER AND SLAVE-CATCHING.

IT may seem strange that the practice of slave-hunting, so much reprehended among human beings, should be instinctively followed by insects, but it is nevertheless the fact that many ants are actually obliged to make slaves in order to live. The species in question can certainly manage without slaves, although it is more comfortable with them. The late Mr. F. Smith found in its nests no less than four other species of ant, all of which were contentedly playing the part of domestic servants. Sometimes they even assail the nests of their own species.

Mr. Bignell showed me a couple of specimens of the Wood Ant, both workers, one of which had been captured by the other, and was being carried into the nest by the captor.

The nest into which the ant was being carried was by far the largest in the neighbourhood, and it really seemed as if its rulers would suffer no rival establishments, and were merging them in the one great central nest.

There are some species of ants which are absolutely dependent on their slaves, and would die but for their help. Such, for example, is the *Polyergus rufescens* of Southern Europe, popularly called the Slave-maker.

This insect carries out to the fullest extent the idea prevalent in the Middle Ages, that labour of any kind is a degradation. Fighting was the only occupation worthy of a noble; and fighting is not simply the only occupation worthy of a Slave-maker Ant, but is the only one which it is able to follow. It can fight most fiercely, but it can do nothing else. On its slave-hunting expeditions it is fierce, active, and formidable. At home it is helpless. It can invade the dwellings of other ants and carry them off as slaves, but without the help of those slaves it would die.

It cannot make its own dwelling, it cannot provide supplies of daily food, it cannot bring up its own young, and, worst of all, it cannot even feed itself, for its jaws, although formidable as weapons, seem incapable of picking up food. All these offices have to be performed by the slaves.

If the creatures multiply and require a fresh dwelling,

the slaves make it for them, and actually carry their masters to the new nest, the latter being incapable of walking to it without their help. The slaves bring in food, and not only feed the larvæ, but their masters also, who, from long disuse, have lost the power of feeding themselves, just as the banana, from constant propagation by slips, has lost the power of producing seeds.

Huber's experiments with this extraordinary ant are too well known to need repetition. I will only mention that when thirty Amazons, with a quantity of larvæ and pupæ, were confined in a box, together with a supply of honey, the insects did not know how to feed themselves, and fifteen died of starvation on the second day. Huber then introduced a single slave. This little creature at once assumed the management, fed the starving Amazons and larvæ, scooped out a dwelling, and helped the newly developed ants out of their pupa cases.

Sir J. Lubbock repeated this experiment, with the exception of allowing the ants to die of hunger, and kept a number of the Amazons in perfect health by lending them a slave for an hour or two daily, in order to feed and cleanse them.

In slavery among ants we see one of the many human attributes which belong to these wonderful insects. Moreover, we have slavery presented to us in its best form. The ants are the kindest of masters to their servants, and the latter are evidently imbued with the warmest attachment to them. In the case already mentioned, the slave was not compelled to feed and " do for" its master, but set about its task with voluntary goodwill. Then the ants are fond of play, and behave just like children.

Anyone who watches an ants' nest may see the insects at play with each other. One of their favourite games is for one ant to pick up another in its jaws, carry it for some little distance, and then put it down. The playmate meanwhile curls itself into a ball, tucks in its legs, and comports itself so that it may be more easily carried.

They keep domestic pets in the form of a tiny species called *Stenamma Westwoodii*. It possesses no popular title, as it is so small—scarcely the tenth of an inch in length—and is only found in the nests of other ants, the Wood Ant seeming to be its favourite host.

"The *Stenammas*," writes Sir J. Lubbock, "follow the Formicas when they change their nest, running about among them, and between their legs, tapping them inquisitively with their antennæ, and sometimes even climbing on their backs, as for a ride, while the larger ants seem to take little notice of them. They almost seem to be the dogs, or, perhaps, rather the cats, of the ants."

The same observer goes on to mention that there is an allied species of much the same size, *Solenopsis fugax*, which harbours in the nests of larger ants, and, instead of being a pet for them, is a deadly foe. It makes its own galleries and tunnels within those of its unwilling hosts, and carries off their larvæ as food. Owing to the small size of its burrows, the plundered ants cannot follow it. In fact, "it is as if we had small dwarfs, about eighteen inches to two feet high, harbouring in the walls of our houses, and every now and then carrying off some of our children into their horrid dens."

The variation in size among ants is, by the way, as well marked as it is among the higher animals, and the proportions of the largest and smallest ant are much the same as those of the elephant and the mouse. Some ants, especially those belonging to the genus *Componotus*, are as large as our hornets, while others, such as the too-common House Ant, *Myrmica molesta*, is only the fifteenth of an inch in length, and so slender that its pale yellow body is hardly discernible if it be alone.

Minute as are its individual dimensions, collectively it is so formidable an insect that it has rendered houses uninhabitable. The houses have had the floors relaid, cement and porcelain tiles used wherever possible, but the House Ants have retained possession of the premises.

I have received many letters from persons whose houses are infested with these ants, and have been asked to suggest some mode of destroying them. Unfortunately, I know of none. The passages to their nests are so small that boiling water loses its heat long before the few drops which can trickle through them can touch the nest. Insect powders are equally useless, and sulphur smoke has no terror for these insects.

Another very human characteristic of the ant is that they take in lodgers.

There are many insects which are never seen except in

the nests of ants. If these lodgers were restricted to the ant tribes it would still be a remarkable custom. But not only do many ants act as lodgers, but beetles of different kinds may be found there, most of them being various species of rove-beetles (*Staphylinidæ*). The beautiful rose-beetle, *Cetonia aurata*, is often to be found there, and, in consequence of this habit, in some places is called the King of the Ants.

Neither is their hospitality confined to insects. The common Yellow Ant, *Formica flava*, receives woodlice into its nest. These rather unexpected guests live in little chambers communicating by passages. If the nest be laid open, even in the severest frosts, and the earth removed to a depth of four inches or so, the woodlice may be found in their apartments, having been perfectly protected from the cold by the few inches of earth above them.

THE MOST GIFTED INSECT RACE.

CHAPTER IV.

FOOD AND FORAGING EXPEDITIONS.

THE food of ants is extremely varied. Mostly it consists of animal substances. Advantage is taken by zoologists of their fondness of animal food. If they want the skeleton of a mouse, rat, snake, frog, lizard, or small bird, they have nothing to do but put it into a tin box perforated with holes, and place the box near a populous ants' nest. The insects are not long in finding it out, and stream in and out of the holes, carrying fragments of food to their nests.

In this way they will clean the bones from every particle of flesh, leaving nothing but the sinews by which the bones are attached to each other. Should the skeleton be that of a bird, the large feathers of the tail and wings will mostly be found adhering to the bones, the ants not having been strong enough to pull them out of their sockets.

Sweet juices of all kinds are much admired by all ants. It is scarcely possible to guard jam and other preserves where the House Ants have gained admission into the store-closet. As to sugar or honey, they will empty the jars in a marvellously short time.

In the hotter parts of the earth, where ant-life attains its fullest development, it is scarcely possible to keep provisions of any kind. The only protection that is of the slightest efficacy is, to place the vessel on a table, and immerse each leg of the table in a basin of water. Even then care must be taken that the water be kept perfectly clean, as if any small floating objects should fall into it, the ants will use them as rafts; and if dust be allowed to accumulate on the surface the insects will crawl over it. They will even scale walls, creep along the ceiling until they are over the table, and then allow themselves to drop upon it.

Many species go on foraging expeditions, which are managed with as much order and discipline as a body of foragers in a modern army. The most redoubtable of these foragers are called Driver Ants, and there are several species of them, each having its own way of foraging. Those which are best known belong to the genus *Eciton*, and inhabit tropical America. In these creatures the division of labour is remarkably carried out, the workers being broadly divided into labourers and soldiers. The latter are very much larger than the former, and act as officers while the column is on the march. Mr. Bates, the well-known traveller, in describing a column of Driver Ants some hundred yards in length, has the following remarks on the officers and their duties :—

"The large-headed individuals were in proportion of about five in one hundred to the small individuals, but not one of them carried anything in its mandibles. They were all trotting along outside the column, and distributed in regular proportions throughout the whole line of army, their globular white heads rendering them very conspicuous among the rest, bobbing up and down as they traversed the inequalities of the road." From such a column a number of branch columns are perpetually thrown out for the purpose of exploring the neighbourhood of the actual line of march.

Another species, *Eciton prædator*, prefers the "flying column," *i.e.* a mass of foragers detached from their base.

These creatures are of inestimable service to the human inhabitants of the country. Snakes, rats, mice, venomous centipedes, scorpions, gigantic cockroaches, &c., swarm in tropical America, and always find their way into houses, whence the inhabitants cannot expel them, but the Driver Ants can and will do so, and consequently the approach of a flying column is hailed with joy.

Its coming is heralded by the appearance of certain birds which feed largely on these ants, and which may be seen perched on the topmost branches of the trees.

As soon as it is seen that the ants are approaching the houses, the inhabitants turn out, previously opening all the doors, boxes, and drawers in the house.

Just as in a military advance, a small vanguard of a single ant makes its appearance, the Uhlan of the ant-army, whereat the "vermin" take alarm and try to escape. But the solitary adventurer is followed by rapidly-increasing bodies of its companions, and the house is filled with ants. They pour in from all sides, penetrate into every crevice, overpower and tear to pieces every living thing on the premises, and then evacuate them in search of fresh prey. Not even a flea is left alive, and for a few months there is peace in the house. These ants generally make their foraging expeditions at the beginning of the rainy season.

Mr. Bates mentions that he has seen the Ecitons ascend the trees, attack the great wasp-nests which hang from the branches, tear them to pieces, and capture and devour the inhabitants. He has also seen them laying siege to the nest of one of the great burrowing ants, sink a mine, pour into the nest by thousands, and drag out the inhabitants. They were so determined and courageous that when Mr. Bates picked up some of the burrowing ants for his collection, the Ecitons actually pulled them out of his fingers.

The perfect organisation of the tunnelling operations in this case was as remarkable as that of the army on the march. The ants divided themselves into two distinct bodies, one digging out the earth and forming it into pellets, and the others receiving the pellets from their comrades and carrying them away.

On such occasions not only are the inhabitants of the nest carried off, but the nest itself is pulled to pieces and the fragments taken to the fortress of the depredators. A double column of ants is always formed for this purpose, one side of the column going towards the nest for the purpose of plundering it of its contents, and the other side going homewards laden with their spoil.

Sometimes these foraging columns are overtaken by the sudden floods which at times pour down from the mountains and sweep over many miles of country. It would seem as if the ant-army must be annihilated, but the insects are equal to the emergency. They cling together in spherical masses, often as large as cricket-balls, and as a quantity of air is entangled among their limbs they float lightly on the surface of the water, and roll over and over in the current, waiting to be washed ashore. The ant-ball then separates, and none of its members are any the worse for their excursion.

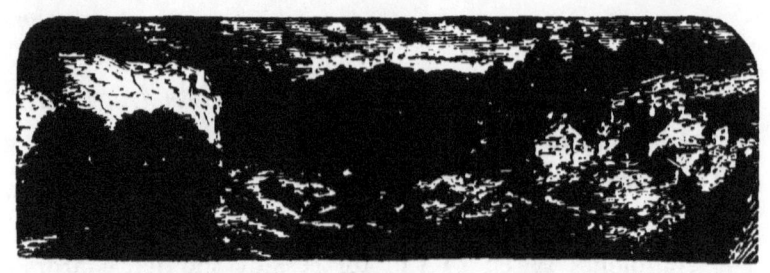

THE MOST GIFTED INSECT RACE.

CHAPTER V.

THEIR ARCHITECTURE.

IN architecture the ants are not so pre-eminently superior as the Termites, or White Ants, as they are wrongly called, but they are wonderful burrowers, and even in our commonest British species the labyrinth of passages and chambers which compose the nest is a marvel to see; but seeing it is extremely difficult, as the ants, however much they may need light in their predatory or military expeditions, banish it utterly from their homes, and detest it.

How the ants can find their way through such a complicated series of galleries, each being to our eyes exactly similar to all the others, is a mystery. Perhaps they may have some mode of guiding themselves independently of light.

It has been said that they know the structure of the nest, and can trace their way by touch, using their antennæ as a blind man does his stick. But they cannot know the construction of other nests, and yet, when one body of ants attacks the nest of another, the invaders plunge boldly into the galleries of the strange nest, and seem to have no difficulty in chasing their inmates through them.

Their eyes have nothing about them especially worthy of attention, except the extremely variable number of the facets. In one species the insects have a thousand facets to each compound eye; but this number is, however, far less than is found in many other insects, especially those butterflies which belong to the genus *Fanessa*.

There seems, indeed, to be little doubt that the ants depend much more on touch than on sight for their guidance. Sir John Lubbock made a series of experiments with some ants, giving them food, and placing it on a wooden cylinder eight inches in height. When an ant had been accustomed to make her way to the honeyed bait, the cylinder was moved only six inches from its former position. The ant, on her return from the nest, was quite bewildered, not appearing to see the cylinder, and only came against it by chance.

The evident inference was that sight was a less valuable guide to the food than some other faculty, which was probably the sense of smell. No experiments have as yet decided the question as to the sense of hearing.

If a further proof of the comparatively small use of sight be needed, it may be found in the Blind Ant (*Eciton erratica*).

This remarkable being has no eyes at all, the horny covering of the head being uniformly smooth, without the least indication of eyes. Yet, like several eyeless beings, the Blind Ant is conscious of light, and dislikes it, never venturing into the open air. It certainly marches for long distances, but always through slight covered ways, which it builds for itself as it goes along.

Whatever may be the sense which guides these insects through their subterraneous tunnels, it is a very acute one, for in some of the species the tunnels are of almost incredible dimensions.

The most notable tunneller among the ants is called scientifically *Atta cephalotes*, and is known by the popular names of Saüba, Parasol Ant, or Umbrella Ant. The specific name of *cephalotes*, or Big-headed, is given to it on account of the enormous heads of the worker-soldiers.

These ants make their nests very much on the same principle adopted by our Wood Ant, *i.e.* there is a domed hillock above-ground, and a vast number of passages underground, connected with the hillock. This external nest is made of leaves, which are brought for the purpose by the small workers.

The leaves being very much larger than the ants which carry them, the latter are quite hidden beneath the green burden. It was at one time thought that the leaves were carried in order to keep the sun's rays off the insect, which was therefore called the Parasol Ant. It is now, however, known that the ant simply holds the leaf aloft, because it is the easiest method of carrying it.

Though the small workers bring the leaves, they are not allowed to lay them. That department is taken by the large-headed workers, who receive the materials but allow none but themselves to arrange them. In fact, the line of demarcation is as strongly shown among ants as among our own bricklayers, none of whom will condescend to carry either hod or mortar, and will not suffer a mere labourer to lay a brick.

The extent of the Saüba's tunnelling is almost incredible, and their galleries often do very much harm in civilised localities. They have been known to pierce an embankment, and cause a flood by letting out the water; and I know of a case where a gold mine in Brazil was totally ruined by the Saübas, which had driven an unsuspected gallery into it just before the rainy season. Accordingly, when the rains came the water rushed in a torrent through the mine, washed away the wooden roof and uprights, destroyed the tram, and not only stopped the progress of the mine, but necessitated the reconstruction of the damaged gallery before the ore could be taken to the "stamps" by which it is broken up for the extraction of the gold.

The modes of obtaining and storing food are as varied as the other habits of the insects. I have mentioned n another volume how our British ants use the aphides like milch cows, taking from them the sweet juice that exudes from two little tubes on the abdomen.

In our country the ants do not store up grain for food, but in many parts of the world the ants not only store up grain, but some of them actually plant it, tend it, reap it, and carry it when ripe into their nests. Mentone is one of the localities of a Harvesting Ant, which is scientifically called *Aphenogaster barbata*. About twenty species of Harvesting Ants are now known. The present species is black, shining, and larger than our wood ant. The most curious point in the economy of this ant is, that it not only stores the grain, but actually converts it into malt. The seeds are allowed to begin sprouting, and the tiny cotyledons are then bitten off, so as to stop the growth. Then the seeds are brought out of the nests and laid in the sun to dry, so that the starch is converted into sugar, and is thus rendered suitable for food.

Another and still more wonderful Harvesting Ant is the Agricultural Ant (*Myrmica barbata*) of Texas. It is about as large as the preceding insect, but is of a yellowish brown colour instead of black.

This insect begins by preparing a field for its intended crop. It raises a flat-topped, circular mound, some seven or eight feet in diameter, and plants upon it the seeds of a peculiar grass. Dr. Lincecum says that after watching these ants for more than twelve years, he never saw them use more than that one species of grass.

The insects keep their ground in beautiful condition, never allowing a weed to show itself, and watching over the seeds until they are ripe. They then cut off the small, white seeds and carry them below, where they separate the husks, throwing the latter away outside their enclosure. Should the weather be wet the ants wait for the first fine day, and carry the seeds into the sunbeams for the purpose of drying them. Sprouting seeds they reject, herein differing from the practice of their European relatives.

An Indian Harvesting Ant (*Podomyrma rufonigra*) is on occasions useful to the natives. In famine years the starving people hunt carefully for the nests of this ant, take out the grain and husks together, and grind them into meal.

"Last scene of all." Not many years ago, if anyone had dared to state that ants not only bury their dead, but pay funeral honours to them, he would have forfeited all claims to credibility. Yet, even this peculiarly human trait of character has been recorded.

A number of ants which had attacked a little boy had been killed, about twenty of them lying dead upon the ground. After a while a procession of ants came from the nest and marched two by two towards their dead companions. Four were told off to each corpse, two carrying it and the other two walking behind. When the bearers were tired they transferred their burden to the second pair, and walked behind the others in their turn. A body of two hundred or so brought up the rear.

On reaching a sandy hillock, about half of them set to work at digging graves for their comrades, one grave for each ant, and the other half laid the bodies in the graves and filled them up with the soil. Six or seven of them would not work, and were set upon and killed by the others. No separate graves were made for them, but a large hole was dug, and the bodies of the delinquents tumbled into it promiscuously. Only the deserving soldiers were accorded the honours of such a funeral. Common labourers were simply buried where they lay, and no funeral procession was formed.

This extraordinary scene was first witnessed at Sydney, New South Wales, and the whole account may be seen in the Journal of the Linnean Society, vol. v., p. 217.

THE MARVEL OF INSECT LIFE.

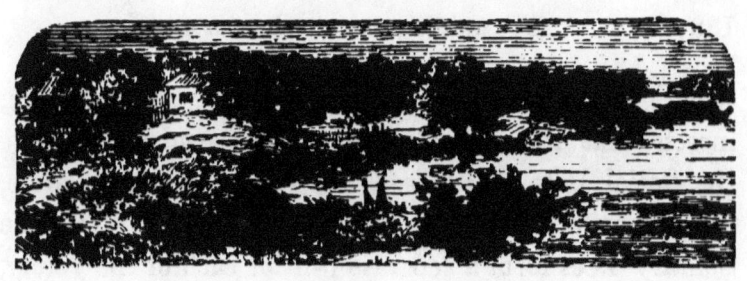

THE MARVEL OF INSECT LIFE.

CHAPTER I.

SOLITARY BEES—THEIR HABITS AND WORK.

THE reader must not expect to find in the following pages a description of the Bee and its management. I shall simply attempt to give an outline history of the various bees all over the world, their habits, and the work which they do. Among them the Hive Bee will find its place, but not as a domesticated insect, these pages treating of the natural, and not the artificial life, of the insects which will be mentioned.

Roughly speaking, we may divide the bees into two great groups, the Solitary and the Social, and will begin with the former.

Like the generality of insects, the Solitary Bees are either male or female, and only the latter possesses a sting. It is an universal rule among sting-bearing insects that the males are perfectly harmless. Unlike the Social Bees, which feed the young grubs, or larvæ, until they are about to assume the pupal state, the Solitary Bees form a separate cell for each of the young, fill it with a supply of food which will nourish it until it becomes a pupa, close up the cell, and leave it.

Chief among them are the Earth-burrowers, many of which belong to the genus Andrena.

Some of them prefer hard soils, and have especial liking for well-trodden paths, the harder and more stony the better. Their holes are very small, and as they burrow to the depth of eight or ten inches, it is not an easy matter to trace their excavations.

The best plan is to insert a flexible grass stem into the hole, and dig a funnel-shaped pit, of which the grass stem occupies the centre. At the end of the tunnel will be found a little cell, simply excavated in the earth and filled nearly to the ceiling with pollen. Generally there is only one cell to each tunnel, but occasionally the bee digs several branch tunnels, and places a store of food and an egg in each. Within this dark subterraneous chamber the egg is hatched into a legless grub, such as has been mentioned. It immediately begins to feed, and as soon as it has finished the pollen heap in which it is placed, it changes into a pupa, and subsequently into a perfect insect.

These bees are very common along the sea-shore, especially where the coast is composed of chalk cliffs above and sand below. Like all bees, they are very fond of salt-water, and may be seen to settle on the sand and drink their briny draught with great zest.

Some of these bees are fond of sand-banks, and one, the Kentish Bee (*Andrena picipes*), is remarkable for the fact that it is almost wholly confined to the county whence it derives its name. The face of any sand quarry in any part of Kent is tolerably sure to contain the tunnels of this bee. It burrows almost horizontally, and does not penetrate to any great depth. The tunnels are generally set closely together, so that I have procured in a few minutes several dozen of the silken cells spun by the larvæ just before their change. The cell at the end of the tunnel is stored with the white pollen of the thistle, and the mother bee has a most curious aspect as she flies to her burrow so laden with pollen that she looks as if she had been rolled in a flour-barrel. When she comes out again she would hardly be recognised as the same insect, the colour being nearly black, with the exception of the second joint, or tibia, of the hind leg, which is silvery white below and brown above.

There is one enormous genus of Solitary Bees called Osmia. These insects make their nest in all kinds of unexpected places. They will utilise nail-holes in garden walls; and I have seen an old stone wall that had once belonged to a garden, literally swarming with these bees. A brick wall is scarcely so much favoured by them, as the bricks are too regularly laid to allow of much excavation between. Some of the Osmia bees are very small, and burrow into the pith of broken or cut twigs. If the ends of some cut branches of a rose, a bramble, or a jessamine be examined, some of them will be found to have a little round hole in the pith scarcely large enough to admit a No. 5 shot. If such twigs be cut longitudinally, they will be seen to contain a row of little oblong cells, from which in process of time will be developed tiny blackish bees. Several insects have this

Fig. 1.—OSMIA BURROWS.   Fig. 2.—MEGACHILE BURROW.

habit, but that which is most commonly found in twigs is *Osmia leucomelana*.

The number of cells is very variable. Sometimes there are six or seven, but in a specimen now before me there are only three. The bee, however, seems to have met some impediment in her work. She has begun, as usual, in the centre of the pith, but, instead of keeping to the middle, she has gone off obliquely until she came against the wood. Then she has gone downwards for a little distance between the wood and the pith, and probably has disliked the direction of the burrow, deposited her eggs in as much of it as was completed, and gone off to make another.

Another species, *Osmia parietana*, which is seldom seen except in the northern parts of England, makes its dwellings under flat stones. There is a wonderful example of these habitations in the British Museum. The stone is only ten inches in length by six in width, and in it are fixed two hundred and thirty-six cells.

They will build in almost any crevice, even choosing such singular spots as a keyhole, an empty bottle, the barrel of a revolver pistol, &c. Some years ago I was at a sale, and the auctioneer offered, among other lots, a large handbox filled with odds and ends. I bought the box, and found among its contents a piccolo flute. In trying its tone it refused to utter a sound, and on looking into it the interior was seen to be stuffed with some soft substance, apparently paper. A closer examination, however, showed that it was completely filled with the cells of an Osmia. The flute can be seen in the nest-room at the British Museum.

Another of these ubiquitous bees, *Osmia bicolor* generally selects the empty shells of the common banded snail, filling them with eggs, honey, and pollen, placing a wall of some vegetable substance between each egg and its neighbour.

Another wall-frequenting bee is called *Megachile muraria*. It makes cells very like those of the Osmia as may be seen by the illustration. These cells were found in the fluting of a pillar.

There are several species of Osmia which do not take the trouble of burrowing, but penetrate into straws, especially those of thatched roofs. They have even been known to find their way into grocers' shops and make their way into maccaroni, much to the disgust of the consumer.

Some of these solitary burrowing bees are known by

Fig. 3.—ROSE-CUTTER BEES AND NEST. (Half actual size.)

the name of Leaf-cutters, because they make their successive cells of the leaves of different trees and shrubs. Rose-leaves are generally chosen by this insect, which cuts semicircular pieces out of the edge of the leaf, carries the severed portions to its burrow, and in a most wonderfully ingenious manner forms them into a series of cells, looking like a number of thimbles thrust into each other. These beautiful nests are not uncommon, but a good specimen is hardly ever seen in a collection, owing to the difficulty of preserving them. It is useless even to attempt to retain the colour, and without the most careful preparation the leaves will become dry, uncurl themselves, and fall asunder.

On the Continent, but not, I believe, in England, an allied insect uses the petals of the scarlet poppy instead of rose-leaves.

One British solitary bee, *Anthidium manicatum*, seems to have been first noticed by Gilbert White, who called it the Hoop-shaver, because it uses its jaws much as a hoop-maker uses his shave.

It makes its burrow in soft wood, generally the "touchwood" found in decaying willow-trees. If, however, it can find the deserted tunnel of a goat-moth caterpillar it will make use of it instead of gnawing a burrow for itself. The cells in which its young are reared are made of the down of various plants, the common campion being apparently the favourite.

Opening its jaws widely, the bee places them against the stem, and, running quickly along it, shaves off the down in a sort of spiral coil which quite covers its head. With this down, mixed with some glutinous substance, it makes the cells for the reception of its young.

The typical wood-boring bee, however, is not known to inhabit England. Its scientific name is *Xylocopa* (*i.e.* wood-cutter) *violacea*. At first sight it looks very much like a large black Humble Bee, but it can easily be distinguished from these insects, not only by the shining abdomen, which is but sparely covered with hairs, but by the deep violet colour of the wings. Popularly it is called the Carpenter Bee; but there are so many bees which

Fig. 4.—XYLOCOPA, OR CARPENTER BEE. (Half actual size.)

deserve this term that neither of them can arrogate it to itself.

This bee is especially remarkable for the solidity of its work. Usually the cells or partition walls of the tunnelling bees are exceedingly fragile, no matter what may be the material of which they are made.

Unlike the generality of burrowing insects, which carry

the excavated material to a distance, so as not to betray the burrow, the Xylocopa reserves a considerable portion of the woody fragments for the purpose of separating her burrow into a series of cells. Having placed a sufficient quantity of food at the bottom of the burrow, and an egg upon the food heap, she takes a number of wood chips, moistening them with saliva, and places them in a ring-like shape just above the food. When the first ring is dry, she makes a second ring within it, and so proceeds until she has made a nearly flat floor of concentric rings. When finished, the floor is about as thick as a penny, and it becomes exceedingly hard as it dries.

Naturally we might think that the eggs which were laid first would hatch first, and that therefore the insect must injure its companions by breaking through their cells in its way to the entrance of the burrow, even if it had sufficient strength for the task. The solution of the problem is beautifully simple, and is thus described by the late Mr. F. Smith, whose knowledge of the Hymenoptera was unrivalled:—"The bees which first arrive at their perfect condition, or rather those which are first anxious to escape into day, are two or three in the upper cells. These are males; the females are usually ten or twelve days later. This is the history of every wood-boring bee which I have bred, and I have reared broods of nearly every species indigenous to this country."

There is another burrowing bee (*Chalicodoma*) which makes partitions in a similar manner. But, as it is an earth-borer, it forms its floors of concentric rings of clay instead of wood chips. It is a native of South Africa.

Before passing to the Social Bees, I must bestow a few lines upon one very common and very interesting British insect. This is scientifically named *Anthophora retusa*, and it is generally accepted as the British type of the Mason Bees. It makes a sort of composite nest, placing its cells in the crevices of rocks, holes in the walls, and similar localities, and covering them with a patch of mud, which looks very much as if it had been flung against the wall by accident, and left to dry there. It serves, however, as a protecting cover for the cells, which are made of little pellets of earth fastened together like the wood chips of the Xylocopa. The cells are rough on the exterior, but smooth and polished on the interior. It is a pretty bee, and can be known by the feathered tips of the middle legs.

THE MARVEL OF INSECT LIFE.

CHAPTER II.

HUMBLE BEES—THEIR HOUSEKEEPING.

HAVING given a rapid sketch of Solitary Bees, we shall now glance at those that are social in their habits. These insects fall naturally into two divisions, namely the Humble Bees and the Hive Bees, of which latter insects there are more species than is generally imagined.

In all these insects we find a new element introduced into their economy. The Solitary Bees consist of males and females, as is the case with most insects. But, in the Social Bees, we find three distinct ranks, if we may use the word. There are the males, which we popularly call Drones, the females, which we term Queens, and the Workers, the last-mentioned insects being the rank and file of the bee army, the males and females being the officers.

Males, however, are comparatively unimportant in bee life, bees, like ants, being essentially a nation of Amazons, and the interest of the community centreing in the workers.

Putting the males on one side, we have now to consider one part of the structure which is common to both

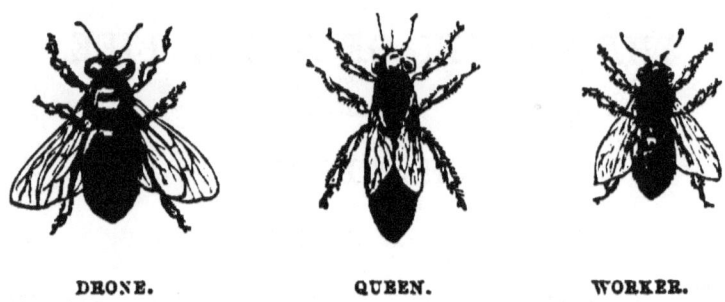

DRONE. QUEEN. WORKER.

the queen and the workers. This is the sting, and a very beautiful apparatus it is.

If we press the abdomen of a bee or wasp, so as to cause the sting to protrude, we should naturally think that the sharp, dark-coloured instrument was the sting itself. This, however, is not the case. The real sting is a very slender instrument, nearly transparent, keenly pointed, and armed on one edge with a row of barbs. So exactly does the sting resemble the many-barbed arrow of certain savage tribes, that if the savages had possessed microscopes, we should certainly have thought that they borrowed the idea of the barb from the insect. What we see with the unaided eye is simply the sheath of the sting.

Many savages poison their spears and arrows. But the sting is infinitely superior to the arrow poison. No poison that has yet been made, not even the terrible wourali, or curare, as it is sometimes called, can retain its strength after long exposure to air. The upas poison of Borneo, for example, loses its potency in two or three

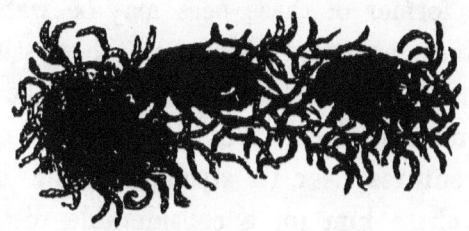

CARDER BEES AT WORK.

hours. But the venom of the sting is never exposed to the air at all. It is secreted by two long, thread-like glands, not nearly so thick as a human hair, and is then received into a little bag at the base of the sting. When the insect uses its weapon, it contracts the abdomen, thereby forcing the sting out and compressing the venom-bag. By the force of the stroke which drives the sting into the foe, its base is pressed against the venom-bag, and a small amount of the poison driven into the wound. As a rule, if the bee or wasp be allowed to remain quiet, it will withdraw its sting, but as the pain generally causes a sudden jerk, the barbed weapon cannot be withdrawn, and the whole apparatus of sting, poison-bag, and glands is torn out of the insect, thereby causing its death.

Three distinct groups of Humble Bee exist in this country, namely, the Meadow Bees, which make their nests underground; the Carder Bees, which build on the surface of the earth; and the Stone Bees, which choose their habitations in the clefts of rocks, stone-heaps, and similar situations.

The two former of these bees may be watched with perfect safety, as they seldom use their stings, even when their homes are invaded. But it will be as well to let the Stone Bee alone. This insect will dash at any one who ventures near its stronghold, and if he runs away, will chase him for a considerable distance. Its sting is thought to be as severe as that of the hornet.

These wild Social Bees all set about housekeeping in much the same way. A female, or "queen," has been hidden throughout the winter in some sheltered spot, and when the warm spring days come, she emerges from her concealment, and flies about in search of a home.

The Wood Humble Bee almost invariably chooses the deserted burrow of a mouse, enlarges and smoothes the extremity of it, and then begins her nest. She provides a store of food, deposits her eggs, makes some rude cells and feeds the young until they are ready to change into pupæ. Each larva then spins for itself an oval cocoon, from which it is relieved at the proper time by the parent, who bites a circular piece from one end, as if it were a previously made lid.

At first, only worker bees are developed, the males and females appearing later in the year. The workers come to the assistance of the queen, who has thenceforth little to do but deposit eggs. They watch over the

HUMBLE BEES AND CELLS.

young larvæ, feed them, fetch honey and store it in the vacant cells, and in fact do all the work of the community. The honey cells are not placed together as is the case with the Hive Bee, but are mixed with the breeding cells, and heaped together without the least attempt at regularity. The honey is, as a rule, very sweet and fragrant, but it is sometimes injurious to human beings.

Here I may mention that no bee can suck honey out of flowers, as is popularly supposed. She licks it out with her tongue, the end of which is covered with hairs, so as to convert it into a brush, scrapes it between the jaws, and so passes it into the crop, where it is changed into honey.

What property there may be in the crop which converts flower juice into honey, we do not at present know. To

CARDER BEES. EXTERIOR OF NEST.

all appearance, the crop is nothing but a bag of exceedingly fine membrane, and yet, after remaining for a little time in the crop, the flower juice undergoes a change in consistence, flavour, and scent, and, whether the insect be a wild or domestic bee, the change is identical throughout. At the end of autumn the males and workers all die, and only one or two of the females appear to survive the winter.

For its nest the Carder Bee is content with a slight

hollow on the surface of the ground, covering it with a low dome of moss, grass, or similar materials. The bee is very careful that all the fibres should be separated so that they may be properly laid, and subjects them to a kind of combing, or "carding" process, drawing them under her body, and passing them through the three pairs of legs. Sometimes, several bees will unite in the

CARDER BEES. INTERIOR OF NEST.

labour, standing in a row and passing the moss or grass from one to the other.

The dome is rendered waterproof by an inner coating of dark, coarse wax, and in most cases it is made with such care that it looks just like a tuft of ordinary moss upon the ground.

THE MARVEL OF INSECT LIFE.

CHAPTER III.

HIVE BEES—THEIR DISCIPLINE AND HARMONY.

ON passing from the wild to the domestic Social Bees, we find a contrast quite as well marked as between a semi-savage and a civilised country. In the one, a sort of happy-go-lucky system prevails, the cells being of no very particular shape, jumbled together without the least attempt at arrangement, space and material being treated as if they were of no consequence, and each bee seeming to act without reference to any other.

In the nest of the Hive Bee, no matter what the species, we find discipline, harmony, subordination of each insect to the wants of the general community, and economy of space and material carried to the last possible extreme. Division of labour is also practised, though not to so great an extent as among the ants, and even the workers are separated into two classes, namely the architects and the nurses. No longer do we find wasted space or material, the latter being far too valuable to the insect. The cells are wholly made of wax, a substance which is not gathered from flowers or trees, as many persons still believe, but is in reality secreted by the insects themselves.

On the under surface of the worker bee may be seen six little flaps, and on lifting them up with the point of

SECTION OF COMB.

a needle the flaps disclose six tiny pockets. Within these pockets the wax is secreted, forming small flakes nearly semicircular in shape. Some time is required for the development of the wax scales, and during that time the bee requires to be at rest. By degrees the pockets are filled, and when the wax flakes show themselves outside the flaps the bee removes them with its jaws, masticating them together, and then places the mass where it will be wanted.

The cells of the Hive Bee are placed nearly horizontally

and in a double row, end to end. They are hexagonal in shape, so as to avoid wasted space, and the bottom of each cell is composed of three diamond-shaped plates, all exactly alike, and fixed to the cell so that they exactly correspond with the bottoms of three cells in the opposite

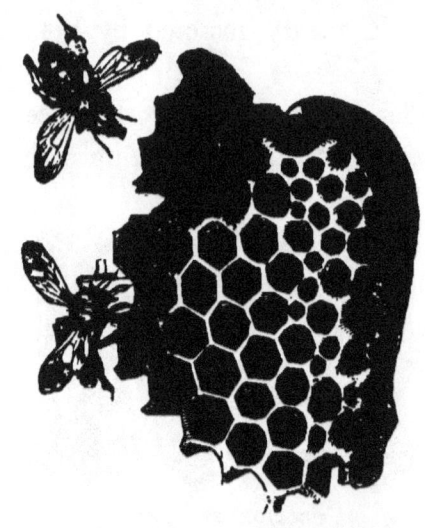

HIVE BEE. EDGE OF COMB WITH ROYAL CELL.

layer. Mutual support is thus given, and the cells are strengthened just where strength is most needed.

If we ask how the bee makes its cells so mathematically perfect, we have no answer. The fact is, that we do not know how the bee builds its hexagonal cell, any more than we know how the termite is taught to rear its gigantic palaces, the caddis-worm to make its subaquatic tubes, the swallow to build its nest of mud, and the sand-martin to burrow holes in soft rocks.

Another remarkable point in bee architecture is the mode in which the edges of the cells are strengthened. The sides of the cells are so exceedingly fragile that even the touch of a passing bee might break their edges if they were not protected with some material harder than wax. Such a material is the "propolis," an adhesive vegetable secretion obtained from various sources, the bud of the chestnut being the chief favourite. By masticating this propolis with wax, the bee forms a tolerably hard cement, with which it guards the edges of the cells, fills up all needless crevices, fastens the edges of the hive to the footboard, and employs for various similar purposes.

Considering the wonderful care which the bees bestow on the ordinary cells, we might naturally imagine that the cells in which the queen bees are bred would be formed with more than double care. But, when we look into the hive, we see that the cells of the hive queen are even more rude and shapeless than those of the Humble Bees.

Drone cells, which are easily distinguished by their superior size, are as scrupulously hexagonal in shape as the ordinary cells. But any lump of wax seems good enough for a queen's cell, provided that it be large enough. These cells are stuck anywhere on the edges of the combs, and in making them the bees seem absolutely regardless of space and material. Several of these rude cells can generally be found in a hive, their usual shape being pear-like, and their exterior covered with little circular hollows where the bees have taken away wax for some other purpose.

Every one who has the slightest practical knowledge of the Hive Bee knows that at certain times of the year the bees increase so rapidly that the hive can no

SWARM.

longer contain them. Several queens are within the hive, and as a hive, like a house, can have but one mistress, successive swarms leave the hive in search of another home, each swarm being accompanied by a queen.

In civilised countries the bees inhabit artificial dwellings, made either of straw or reed. These "hives" being tolerably uniform in their dimensions, we can form a fairly correct calculation as to the number of swarms which a healthy hive will produce in a season.

In uncivilised countries, where the bees make their habitations in hollow trees, the clefts of rocks, or similar localities, the swarming is very uncertain, depending on the size of their habitations. A curious illustration of this fact occurred in a Wiltshire village where I lived for some years. A swarm of bees had managed to evade their rightful owner, and had made their way into the church roof, between the tiles and the lath-and-plaster ceiling with which most village churches were afflicted at that period. Being undisturbed, the bees increased mightily, but they never sent out a swarm. As long as they restricted themselves to the roof, they were allowed to remain untouched. But after some years, they found their way through the flimsy ceiling, and came into the church in such numbers that the congregration hardly dared to enter the building.

At the beginning of winter, when all the bees were torpid, an entrance was made into their domains, and a wonderful sight it was. The beams and rafters were hidden under the masses of comb. The workmen thought that they had a valuable prize of wax and honey, but they were quite mistaken. In our artificial bee-houses we can induce the insects to store the honey in separate portions of the hive. But in this instance the bees had so much space at command that they mixed

P

up the honey cells with the bread cells and breeding cells, so that the labour of separating them would not have been repaid by the results.

I have already mentioned that there are several species of Hive Bees, but can only give a very brief notice of two. One of these is the Banded Bee of the Nile district (*Apis fasciatus*). This bee is remarkable for the fact that the hives are placed in boats and taken along the course of the river so as to secure a constant supply of food, the owner of the bees paying the owner of the boat by a percentage of wax and honey. The next is the bee, or rather group of South American bees, called "Angelitos," or little angels, because they never sting. Some of them can and do bite fiercely. They, however, possess no poison; and although the bite inflicts a momentary pang, it can do no more.

THE MARVEL OF INSECT LIFE.

CHAPTER IV.

HONEY BEES—THE PRINCIPLE OF ORDER.

DEBÔRAH, "She who speaketh," is the Hebrew name of the Honey Bee, and many-tongued, she speaks many things, preaching sermons without words to those who will hear.

It must be understood that I do not intend to treat of bee-keeping, or of the artificially modified life of the domesticated insect.

In the first place, the subject could not be comprised within my present limits; and in the next, even the proverbial disagreement of doctors is concord itself when compared with strife among bee-masters, who only seem to agree upon one point, namely that all outsiders are inferior beings, and scarcely within the pale of civilisation.

First there is the battle of the hives, which rages incessantly. The advocates for wooden hives ask sarcastically whether bees, when at liberty, make their nests in trusses of straw or in hollow trees? Their opponents retort that hollow trusses of straw are not found lying about, and that if they were, the bees would build in them in preference to any other material. But not being able to find straw, they are forced to put up with hollow trees or rock crevices.

Then comes the dispute about the shape of the hives, which involves the great ventilation question, management of swarms, and a multitude of similar controversies.

So I shall touch upon none of these questions, and though for convenience' sake I use the words "hive" and "hive-bee," I do not intend to treat of "Debôrah," the Speaker's, artificial existence, but of those points of her structure and mode of life which form the texts of her wordless sermons.

First, she preaches Order, without which labour is in vain.

Nothing more orderly can be conceived than the internal economy of the hive. Chief among the bees is the Queen, who has but one task to perform, namely, to deposit eggs from which the future generation will be hatched. So valuable is her life, that it is prolonged for no less than five times the length of a worker bee's life,

HONEY BEES—THE PRINCIPLE OF ORDER. 213

she living four years, and the working bee only nine months. But she has to mature and deposit about eight hundred thousand eggs, each egg having to be placed in a separate cell. If, like many insects, she only needed to drop the eggs on some convenient spot, she would, like them, pass but a brief winged life. But each requires separate attention, and though the queen does nothing for six months of each year but

HONEY BEES AT WORK.

go from cell to cell putting an egg in each cell, the deposition of eight hundred thousand eggs cannot be accomplished in less than the four years which have therefore been allotted to the queen.

The male bee, commonly called the Drone, does no work, and therefore is allowed but a very brief space of existence.

As to the Worker bees, each has its own special task, and although when a number of bees are seen at work, inextricable confusion seems at first to reign, a careful inspection soon shows that the vast multitude is governed by the supremest order, and that, like soldiers in the field or sailors on board their ship, each individual has its own place and its own work.

Some of these workers are told off for the purpose of secreting wax, while others undertake the task of receiving the wax as it is produced, kneading it until it is sufficiently plastic, and rearing the wonderful aggregations of double cells which we call "combs."

Other bees, again, attend on the queen, surround her wherever she goes, feed her, and take care that every egg that she lays is placed in a suitable cell. Another set of bees act as nurses, taking upon them the charge of the young grubs as soon as they are hatched, and feeding them until they are ready for their change into the intermediate or pupal stage of existence.

A fifth order of worker bees go abroad to collect the sweet juice of flowers and transform it into honey in their crops, or to gather the pollen from ripened anthers, carry it home in the wonderful elastic baskets with which their hind legs are furnished, and knead it into "bee-bread" as food for the young grubs.

Some bee-masters think that each of these varied tasks is performed by bees which are destined for it from the time when they are hatched, just like the system of castes among the Hindoos.

Others, of equal experience, think that each bee takes the whole of these labours in rotation, the nature of the task depending on the age of the bee. Thus, the first work of a bee is secretion of wax. Next comes the cell-building, then the nursing of the young, then the attendance on the queen, and lastly the foraging for food.

Be this as it may, the result is the same, and the principle of Order is equally maintained.

There is but one head of the bee-household. In order to provide for the continuance of the race, a number of queens are successively developed; but only one can reign, and as soon as the original queen finds that a successor is at hand, she gathers round her a multitude of her subjects—some thirty or forty thousand in number—and, accompanied by them, sallies forth to found a new colony.

Here again is the principle of Order carried out in the most perfect manner.

Were it not for this all-pervading principle of Order, the singularly complicated economy of the hive could not be maintained.

On an average, in a moderately-sized community,

there are at least fifty or sixty thousand cells to be made, and the wax to be secreted for them. Most of them are "worker" cells, but there is a larger kind in which the male grubs are hatched, called "drone" cells; and then there are the huge supplementary edifices, called "royal" cells, in which the queens are nurtured.

About two thousand eggs are laid daily, and have to be distributed into separate cells.

About twenty thousand grubs must be fed continually, sealed down when they are ready to change into the pupal stage, and set free when they are fully developed. Fully twenty thousand cells must be filled with honey, and perhaps half as many with bee-bread.

Then there are the setting and relieving of sentinels, the hive to be kept scrupulously clean, the ventilation and temperature to be regulated, the provision for successive swarms and their monarchs, and a variety of miscellaneous duties, all of which offices must be carefully arranged, lest any of the bees engaged in them should interfere with each other.

THE MARVEL OF INSECT LIFE.

CHAPTER V.

THE MYSTERY OF HONEY AND WAX.

HERE is the chemistry of Nature's alembic, and the Bee may well preach that she, like ourselves, is "fearfully and wonderfully made."

Every one has seen honey and wax, and most people have seen the honeycomb with the honey in it. But who thinks of the mysteries of honey and wax? Who asks himself *how* they are made? Who reflects that the conversion of flower-juices into honey is at present an insoluble problem to the most advanced of our chemists.

Take any sweet juice you like, whether obtained from flowers, or fruits, or the sugar cane. Pour it into an air-tight receptacle made of any kind of membrane, keep it as long as you think fit, and it will be unchanged.

Let the bee take all or either of these substances, pour it into a little air-tight membranous bag, and when she pours it out again it will be converted into honey, totally differing in flavour, odour, and many other qualities, from the juices from which it was made. Yet the crop, or honey-bag, in which it was kept for a short time, is nothing but a little sac of membrane, so delicate that all its contents can be seen through it, without visible glands by which any additional substance could be secreted, and having no aperture by which any such substance could be introduced into it.

The conversion of sweet juices into honey is a task which at present has totally baffled human efforts, though it is constantly achieved in countless myriads of bees by the Divine chemistry of creation.

So with the wax.

This remarkable substance is not made by the bee, but is secreted. On the under surface of the insect's abdomen there are six little flaps, covering six corresponding membranous pockets, and in them, by some mysterious process, the wax is secreted.

That it is formed, more or less directly, from the food, is evident from the fact that its quality depends much on the nature of the food eaten by the insect which produces it. The best and most tenacious wax is that which is formed by the honey-fed bee, whereas the wax of bees which have fed on sugar is apt to be brittle, and is not so valuable.

There is no apparent connection between the digestive

WAITING FOR THE BEES SWARMING.

system and the wax-pockets. None has as yet been discovered, and although I have dissected many hundreds of bees (some of which are now in the Anatomical Museum at Oxford), I have failed to discover the slightest connection between the food and the wax.

The insects possess neither heart, arteries, nor veins, the blood passing through a valved tube extending along the back, and therefore called the "dorsal vessel," and thence being forced through all the tissues of the internal structure without needing any definite passages through which it is conveyed.

These wax-pockets are only to be found in the worker bees, neither the drone nor queen possessing them.

It is evident that the secretion of the wax is a voluntary process, the bees producing it when needed, and avoiding the strain on their systems when they do not require it. Yet so enormous is the wax-producing power of the bee, that into Russia alone twelve thousand tons are annually imported, the greater part of which is consumed in the wax candles which are so profusely used in the ritual of the Greek Church.

Then take a magnifying glass, and look at the tools by which the insect is enabled to collect and convey to the comb the stores of liquid honey and solid pollen.

For the former purpose, the inner jaws of the bee are greatly lengthened, and contain between them the tongue, which, in spite of its minute size, is as flexible and as much under control as the proboscis of the elephant.

The multitudinous joints of which it is composed are

each furnished with bristle-tufts, so that the whole apparatus when magnified looks very much like a chimney-sweeper's brush greatly elongated, and possessing the advantage of being completely under the control of the owner. With this brush the bee sweeps the sweet juices out of a flower, and scrapes them through its jaws into its mouth, so as to pass them into the crop, where they are converted into honey.

Now transfer the magnifying lens to the hind limbs of the worker bee, and another marvellous structure will be seen.

The middle joint of the leg, technically named the "tibia," is widened and hollowed so as to form a sort of spoon, highly polished in the interior. Round the edges of the hollow are set a number of rather long, stiff, and very elastic bristles. A simple and very effective basket is thus produced, in which the grains of pollen can be conveyed to the hive.

Besides the pollen, another substance is carried in the basket. This is the "propolis," or hard, gummy material which is used as a cement for fastening one part of the hive to another, and also for strengthening the edges of the cells. The propolis is obtained from the viscid adhesive secretions of the chestnut, poplar, birch, and other buds.

THE MARVEL OF INSECT LIFE.

CHAPTER VI.

LET NOTHING BE LOST.

IN the hive nothing ever is wasted, and the most striking example of this fact is the manner in which the wax is used.

This material, being the product of slow secretion from the body of the bee, and demanding that the insect shall do nothing at all during the process, is far too precious to be wasted, and, in consequence, the largest possible result is produced with the least possible expenditure of material. It has been calculated that two pounds weight of wax will suffice for the construction of eighty thousand cells, each cell being separately formed and having its own walls.

How such a structure can be formed, requiring so very

small a weight of wax and yet capable of containing a very great weight of honey, is a problem which will be presently mentioned.

Were it not for the bee, we should be ignorant of one of the uses of flowers, and although we might be delighted with their beauty of form and colour, and charmed with their perfume, could form no idea of their value as producing food for man, as well as the wax without which so many arts and industries could have no existence.

But then comes the bee preacher with her wordless sermon, "Let nothing be lost." She carries the juice to her home, and there transmutes it into the honey and wax which are not only necessary to her own community, but render such inestimable service to mankind.

The amount of annual waste in this country from neglecting the summons of the bee preacher is almost incalculable. An experienced farmer lately put the point in a very terse and simple manner. When speaking of a clover crop, he said that in every ton of clover that was mown, at least seven shillings' worth of honey alone was wasted in the juices which were not removed because there were not sufficient bees to take them.

How much work the bee can do when she has access to suitable flowers may be seen from the fact that, in a single hive, the bees put twenty pounds weight of honey into the combs in forty-eight hours. In such a hive the daily amount of consumption by the inhabitants is about two pounds, so that on the whole the bees carried twenty-four pounds weight of honey into the hive

PLACING THE SWARM IN THEIR NEW HIVE.

within that very limited period. Putting aside the value of the wax, and only counting the honey at its wholesale price, here is at least a guinea's worth of honey made in two days by labourers who want no wages and provide their own food.

When Job, more than three thousand years ago, wrote of "rivers and streaming brooks of honey," and of the "sweet influences of the Pleiades," the starry belt of Orion, the "twelve signs (Mazzaroth) and their seasons," and "Arcturus with his sons," he could have formed no idea of the intimate connection between the vastness of the starry heavens and the tiny cell of the insect that furnished him with "honey out of the rock."

Nor, until the last few years, was the connection of the bee with astronomy known, and then it was discovered by an accident. As this is not a scientific treatise, I cannot go into details, and will only give a very slight account of this important discovery.

It had long been known that the bee-cell possessed the maximum of capacity with the minimum of material, and the cells being placed in double tiers, it was also found that their ends terminated in three diamond-shaped plates uniting in a point which exactly coincided with the centre of the opposite cell, so that each cell gave support to all those surrounding it, and was supported by them in like proportion.

That the mystery of the cell lay in the angles of these plates had been long suspected, and accordingly they were carefully measured, the measurements proving identical, no matter who was the observer.

At last a Scotch mathematician named Maclaurin bethought himself of investigating the mathematical table as well as the bee-cell, and found that in those tables by which astronomers had calculated the courses of the heavenly bodies, and the navigators directed the track of their ships, there was a mistake of a single figure. This single error was sufficient to invalidate all preceding astronomical predictions, and to wreck the vessels that were guided by them.

So here we are brought face to face with the fact that the Creator knows no distinction between small and great.

> "He made the atom and He made the universe,
> And both are equal—both are infinite."
>
> BAILEY.

He employs one and the same means to rule the incalculable vastness of the universe, and to take care that nothing be wasted on this little orb of earth, not even a grain of honey in the cell of a bee.

THE MARVEL OF INSECT LIFE.

CHAPTER VII.

BEES SPEAK A LANGUAGE.

HEBRAISTS say that the name of Debôrah, or "She who speaketh," was given to the bee on account of the humming sound made by its wings in flight. Whether this be so I do not pretend to decide. But it is quite certain that bees do speak a language of their own, and that much of it is not only audible to human ears, but intelligible to human minds.

For example, any one who is accustomed to bees can distinguish between the differing sounds of the wings. There is the quiet hum of contentment. There is the flurried buzz of bewilderment, heard when bees suddenly find themselves without their queen. There is the quick, excited buzz of hunger, and even those who have but little practical acquaintance with bees cannot fail to understand the sharp menacing hum of anger, and to take themselves away as fast as possible.

Anatomists can appreciate this point in the bee's history more than those who have never dissected an insect, because they are completely puzzled as to the production of results with such apparently inadequate means. The wings of insects are not limbs, nor are they moved directly by muscles and tendons, as are the legs. They are attached directly to the thorax, the interior of which is furnished with a multitude of simple muscular fibres, crossing and recrossing much like the warp and woof of a woven fabric.

Physicists see also that the hum of the bee is connected with the theory of acoustics, and know that by means of the instrument called the Siren the number of vibrations per second of a bee's wing can be counted with absolute certainty

Besides the sound produced by the wings, there is the remarkable language employed by the queens shortly before their emerging from the cell. I have already mentioned that when a hive becomes overstocked the queen goes off and takes with her a swarm of her subjects, a new queen being ready in a cell to take her place. These cells are big, shapeless lumps of wax, always stuck on the edge of the comb, lest they should interfere with the symmetry of the ordinary cells.

When the young queen is nearly ready to take her place as head of a community, she begins to utter a series of faint barking sounds, which have been likened to the syllable "Off! off!" very sharply spoken. After a few days she changes the bark into a piping sound, which is accepted as a signal that she is about to make her appearance.

Should, as sometimes happens, the outgoing queen and swarm not be ready to start, the nurse bees that surround the royal cell stop her piping, literally hushing her into silence. Should she disregard them and force her way out too soon, the old queen is sure to attack her, and in all probability both are killed.

Here, then, we have a definite language spoken by the bee and intelligible to man.

I might multiply similar examples to any extent, but the limits of space prevent me from continuing the history of this wonderful insect any further. Suffice it to say that the whole life of the bee, from the moment when it is hatched to the time when its earthly task is finished, is a sermon on one comprehensive text—"The Spirit of God hath made me, and the breath of the Almighty hath given me life."

ABOUT SPIDERS AND THEIR WEBS.

ABOUT SPIDERS AND THEIR WEBS.

CHAPTER I.

LAND SPIDERS.

MOST persons seem to think, or rather, they take for granted without thinking, that a spider is a spider, and that the spider which spins its geometrical web in the branches, or runs over the ground, is identical with the author of the "cobwebs" which have troubled housekeepers for unknown generations.

In reality, even in this country, we have several distinct classes of spiders. There are the Wolf spiders, the Leopard or Hunting spiders, the Crab spiders, the Tube spiders, and so on. Then there are the Gossamer spiders, the Garden spiders, besides the Water spiders, of which we shall give an account.

We will begin with the well-known Garden spider,

Diadem spider, or Cross spider (*Epeira diadema*). Every one is familiar with the flat, circular, wheel-like webs woven by this spider, and I shall therefore content myself with noting a few points as to its economy.

In the first place, there is a bold difference between

THE GARDEN SPIDER.

the threads which form the radiating spokes of the web, and the long, delicate thread which is wound spirally upon the spokes. The former threads are comparatively thick and strong, and if touched with a pin or needle do not adhere to it. The latter thread is very fine in proportion to the spokes, and is adhesive in its character, as passing flies know to their cost. Its adhesiveness is due to little globules of gummy matter, which are arranged upon the thread like beads on a string. These little gum-beads can be rubbed off by careful manipulation, and then the thread is found to be no longer adhesive. A tolerably powerful pocket-lens will show these beads.

On hot, dry, windy days, dust is apt to adhere to the gum, and so impair its adhesiveness. The spider is well aware of this fact, and is constantly employed in clearing the web from dust, using for this purpose the comb-like bristles of the feet.

The mode in which the spider constructs its web is sufficiently curious. It travels round and round, trailing behind it a thread, which is guided by one of the hind legs. As it passes each spoke, it hitches the spiral thread upon it with a sharp regular movement, which much resembles the quick turn of a knitter's forefinger. The thread is always held diagonally across the web, and when it is attached to the spoke, its own elasticity draws it straight.

Were it not for the elasticity of the silk, the spider could not maintain its web, nor get its living. The web is attached to leaves and twigs, which are swayed about by every breath of air, so that they would tear the web to pieces were it not so exceedingly elastic.

Even the struggling of a moderately large fly would tear the web if its material were not elastic. But, as it is elastic as well as adhesive, the insect is detained long enough to enable the spider to seize and kill it.

Sometimes the victim is strong enough to make the spider fear to grapple it in the usual way. In such cases, it casts a cloud of silken fibres over the insect, and by means of its forelegs rolls it over and over, enveloping it so completely that it cannot be seen through its silken shroud. Here, again, the elasticity of the silk comes into operation, and holds the captive so firmly that even a bee or a wasp has no chance of escaping, but is utterly helpless, with its wings and legs swathed firmly to the body.

Another curious example of this elasticity may sometimes be seen on stormy days, when the wind is so violent as to threaten destruction to the webs.

The spider begins by attaching additional "guy" ropes in different directions, but if these should not be sufficient, it has recourse to a singularly ingenious expedient. Attaching a thread to the lower part of the web, the spider lowers itself to the ground, where it searches for a piece of stick or a stone which it thinks suitable for its purpose. Carrying this burden to the thread by which it had lowered itself, it ascends a few inches, fastens the stone to the thread, and then leaves it swinging in the air.

No better plan could be adopted by the most experienced engineer, and it is wonderful to see how exactly the spider adapts the weight to the work which it has to perform.

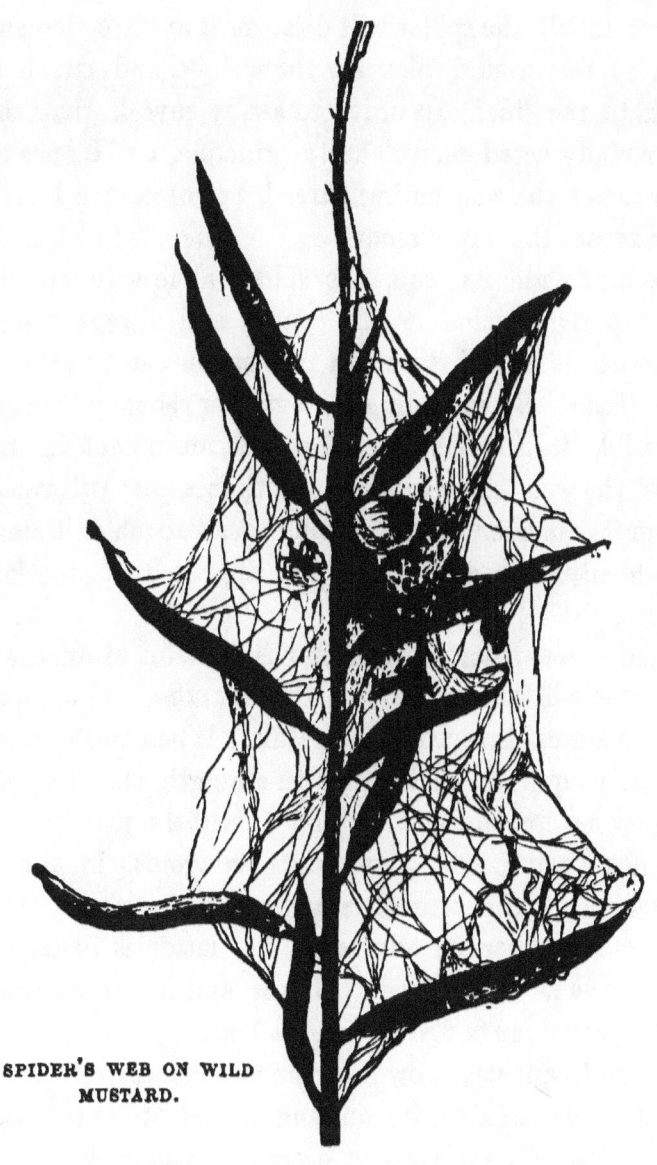

SPIDER'S WEB ON WILD MUSTARD.

If the suspending rope be severed, and the weight be

allowed to fall, the spider will discover it at once, descend again to the ground, pick up the weight, and attach it afresh to the line. In order to assure myself that the spider really acted on a definite principle, I did once or twice break the suspending thread, but of course I shall never repeat the experiment.

Having made its web, the spider almost invariably takes up its position in the centre, and always places itself with its head downwards, if a spider can be said to have a head. By spreading its legs over as many threads as possible, it is able to feel the least movement in any part of the web. The touch of the tiniest gnat will rouse it from its quiescence, but nothing seems to make it start so suddenly into activity as the approach of another spider.

Should one spider trespass on the domains of another, the owner will at once dart at the intruder, and a fierce battle is almost invariably the result. When two spiders are nearly equal to each other in strength, the struggle is a very severe one, each trying to act the part of the ancient retiarius, and envelop its antagonist in a net. When one of the combatants succeeds in casting the silken meshes over its adversary, the latter is instantly rolled up so as to render it helpless, and not until then are the poison-fangs driven into its body.

Not unfrequently, however, the victor receives a fatal wound while making its onslaught, and in that case, after rolling up its adversary, it crawls to another part of the web, gathers its legs close to its body, droops, and dies.

Then, there are many spiders which catch their prey in webs, although they do not weave such beautifully symmetrical structures as those of the Garden spider. The House spiders, for example, belong mostly to the genus *Tegenaria*, the commonest species being *Tegenaria domestica*.

Of course, it is necessary to remove the webs of these spiders from our dwellings, but they should not be disturbed in barns and outhouses, where they can offend no one, and are rather useful than otherwise.

Their webs are well worthy of examination. They are made in horizontal sheets, which are supported by strong threads radiating in different directions. Sometimes, when the conditions are favourable, these sheets attain extraordinary dimensions. The largest that I ever saw were on the roof of the old belfry chamber at Merton College, Oxford. They were destroyed when the building was restored, and I could not examine them, but the smallest must have been several yards square.

One side of the net is always modified into a stout silken tube, in which the spider can sit and watch for prey, itself remaining unseen. Sometimes the spider attains an enormous size, the largest instances known being the celebrated "Cardinal" spiders of Hampton Court. I have had a specimen the spread of whose legs was nearly equal to that of a human hand, and still larger examples have been known. These huge spiders may be found in several parts of England, but they seem to attain their largest dimensions at Hampton Court.

R

Allied species prefer the heaths and commons, and spread their sheets of web over the tops of furze, heather, and similar plants. The eggs of these spiders are enclosed in cocoons of snowy whiteness, which are fastened to the plants. Lest, however, the whiteness of the cocoon should betray it, the surface is always covered with earth, pieces of dead leaves, &c.

There are many spiders which do not entrap their prey in webs, but catch it in fair chase.

These are of two very distinct kinds, called Wolf spiders, and Hunting, or Leopard spiders.

The former are of moderate size, blackish-brown in colour, and may be seen running about the ground with some speed. There are at least sixteen species of British Wolf spiders, all possessing similar habits.

The largest of our British species feeds chiefly on bees belonging to the genus Andrena, and has therefore been named *Lycosa andrenivora*.

A Continental species of Wolf spider is very celebrated under the name of Tarantula (*Lycosa tarantula*), being thought to cause a singular disease consisting of two opposite extremes, profound melancholy and fierce excitement, the latter serving as a sort of channel through which the former was conducted out of the system.

Music was supposed to induce the violent symptoms, and if it could be kept up for a sufficiently long time, the patients became thoroughly exhausted, broke out into a violent perspiration, fell asleep, and when they awoke, were perfectly cured. One tune, familiar under the

SPIDER'S WEB IN OATS.

name of "Tarentella," was thought to have a special efficacy in such cases.

In Jamaica and Australia, the name of Tarantula is mostly applied to various species of trap-door spider. And, as if to increase the error, the Australian colonists persist in pronouncing the word as Triantelope.

The commonest British Wolf spider is called *Lycosa campestis*, and may be seen running about our fields and lawns. In the summer time, the female always has a little globular packet of eggs, done up in a silk bag. This burden she instinctively cherishes even at the risk of her life, but she has so little discrimination that if the bag be taken from her, and a little ball of cotton-wool laid in her way, she will pick it up, carry it about, and be perfectly satisfied.

Some species of Wolf spider haunt the edges of ponds and sluggish ditches. They can run along the surface for the purpose of seizing their prey, and even crawl down the stems of aquatic plants to some depth, carrying with them sufficient air for respiration. They do not, however, dive, like the genuine Water spider.

The really beautiful Hunting spiders may be known by their variegated bodies, which are striped with white or yellow on a dark ground. From this colouring they derive the popular names of Leopard spider, or Zebra spider. They are rather flat-bodied, small, and can be at once recognised by their quick, jerking movements.

Hunting spiders are mostly to be found on walls with a sunny aspect, evidently because flies haunt such spots.

Indeed, in the summer time it is hardly possible to find such a wall without a number of Hunting spiders upon it.

When the spider catches sight of a fly on the wall, it crouches down as low as possible, just like a cat or tiger, and like these creatures, is curiously indistinguishable in spite of its colouring. By very slow degrees, it draws itself towards the fly, and when it comes within distance of its spring, leaps upon it and kills it in a moment. It can leap in this way even though it be on a perpendicular wall. If it be examined closely it will be seen to draw behind it a safety line of silk. The thread is exceedingly delicate, and would escape observation if not sought for.

Every one who has enjoyed the luxury of an early walk on a fine summer day, will have noticed that the ground is sometimes covered with delicate spider webs which have appeared as if by magic, and are covered with tiny dew-drops, which sparkle in the sun like so many diamonds. These are the webs of the Gossamer spider.

The tiny spiders which are popularly called "Money-spinners," because they are supposed to bring good fortune to those persons on whose clothes they spin their almost invisible webs, are mostly Gossamers, and their mode of action, as observed by the best naturalists, is as follows:—The little spider always chooses a hot, fine day, and then climbs to the top of a plant or twig, and emits a long silken thread, which floats loosely in the air. As every one knows, the rays of the sun heat the earth, and cause undulating waves of warm air to ascend continually from it. The floating thread comes across one of these air waves, and when the spider feels itself

MONEY-SPINNERS.

pulled upwards, it loosens its hold of the plant and soars aloft, upborne on the air.

Thousands upon thousands of little spiders thus take their aerial excursions, and when their parachute-threads become interlaced, they form large, loose, irregular sheets of silken web. Sometimes the air is filled with these webs as far as the eye can reach, and any one who happens to be abroad at the time will be quite covered with web and Money-spinners.

The same laws which caused them to rise, regulate their descent. Moisture is always more or less present in the air, and the Gossamer webs take it up, though in the form of invisible vapour. But, when they come across a stratum of colder air, the moisture is at once condensed in tiny globules along their threads, and its weight brings them gently to the ground.

ABOUT SPIDERS AND THEIR WEBS.

CHAPTER II.

THE VENOM-BEARERS—THE BIRD SPIDER.

IN this country there are but few venomous animals, and perhaps only one which could even endanger human life. Yet there are some which are really venom-bearers, and which, although they will not go out of their way to bite or sting, are yet capable of inflicting painful wounds.

Among them may be classed the spiders. We all know that the venom-fangs of spiders are almost instantaneously fatal to insects, and even to their own kind, and it is but natural to suppose that they can be injurious to animals. Very seldom, however, do we find a spider powerful enough to make its venom felt, but now and then a female garden spider of abnormal size will be able to pierce a delicate skin, and to inflict a wound scarcely less painful than that of the wasp or bee.

On the Continent there are plenty of spiders—notably the Tarantula, about which so many absurd stories are told—which will bite fiercely if irritated; but if we wish to see spiders which can kill and feed upon vertebrated animals, we must go to the tropics.

Chief among them is the gigantic Bird spider (*Mygale avicularia*) of tropical America. It is an enormous creature, occupying with outstretched legs a space which a human hand can scarcely cover, and each leg being of great strength.

I have been fortunate enough to see one of these huge spiders alive. It declined to spread itself, but sat with the legs so closely doubled up that the body was almost hidden by them. The body and legs are covered with thick, rather coarse hairs of a reddish brown colour, which even extend over the enormous basal joints of the poison-fangs. In all the group of spiders to which this formidable creature belongs, the fangs are set vertically, so as to strike downwards into the prey, just as do the fangs of a venomous snake.

These poison-fangs are so large and strong that they are sometimes set in gold, as is done with tiger-claws, and are used as toothpicks, their touch being thought to be a preventative against toothache.

The Bird spiders inhabit burrows which they dig in the earth, several inches in depth, and lined with a web so strong that it has been compared to white muslin,

THE BIRD SPIDER.

They do not content themselves with insect prey as do most spiders, but hunt after and kill the smaller lizards and young birds. The Anolis lizard (which the colonist will persist in calling by the name of chameleon), is a very favourite prey of the Bird spider, and so are the young of various humming-birds.

Mr. H. W. Bates, whose travels in the Amazon region are so well known, states that he saw a spider engaged in the destruction of two small finches. One of them was already dead, and was entangled in the broken web, while the spider was still crouching upon the body of the other.

He then proceeds as follows:—"On the extensive plains of Santarem there are hundreds of their broad, slanting burrows. These localities are almost destitute of insects, but they swarm with small lizards and birds, upon which the Mygale seems to feed."

I asked Mr. Bates about these wonderful spiders, and he mentioned a rather curious fact regarding them.

The natives are very fond of pets, and tame monkeys and birds are always to be seen about their huts. Children, however, have a strong fancy for making a pet of the Bird spider, tying a string round its body, and leading it about as if it were a kitten.

Another traveller states that the Bird spider burrows in loose soil, especially that formed by decomposed lava, and issues from its burrow at night in search of prey. He describes it as being a most courageous creature, fighting to the very last, and not being deterred from its attacks even when repeatedly pierced through the body.

The female Mygale is, like our own Wolf spiders, a most devoted parent. She encloses her eggs in a very strong cocoon of white silk, and carries it about with her by means of the appendages called "antennulæ," so that it is protected by her body.

On an average, each cocoon contains nearly two thousand eggs, so that the spiders might be expected to multiply at a rate which would make them masters of the land. However, the balances of nature are always held level, and the counterweight in this case is to be found in the predaceous ants which swarm in the country of the Mygale, and whenever they come upon a cocoon of eggs, or a brood of newly-hatched young, will devour them all, as well as the parent. "One thing," as Solomon says, "is set over against another."

ABOUT SPIDERS AND THEIR WEBS.

CHAPTER III.

TRAP-DOOR SPIDERS.

THE Bird spiders are, I believe, restricted to tropical America, but in many parts of the world there are spiders which burrow in the earth, hunt for their prey after a similar fashion to the Bird spiders, and bring it to their burrows when captured. These creatures also line their burrows with silk, but are far better architects than their larger kinsfolk, inasmuch as they fit up their earthen dwellings with self-closing doors.

The mode in which a Trap-door spider constructs its house is as follows :—

Always choosing a sloping bank, the spider sinks a burrow some five or six inches in depth, and about wide enough to admit a man's forefinger.

Spider's webs are in this country proverbially fragile and delicate. We speak metaphorically of brushing away difficulties like spiders' webs; and the almost invisible fibres spun by very small spiders, such as we call "money-spinners," are used for the cross "wires" of astronomical and other optical instruments on account of their exceeding fineness.

All the Trap-door spiders are remarkable for the great strength of their webs, which are used, not for the capture of prey, but for the strengthening of their earthen homes. The silk is mostly yellow, and so tough that a nest can be removed without any danger of damaging it; and the silk is so strong that even when the earth has been dried and wholly removed, it will bear a considerable strain without breaking, and can be drawn over the finger like a glove.

Up to this point the burrow possesses no advantage over that of the Bird spider, being a simple silk-lined tube. But the spider now sets to work at the construction of a door, by which the opening may be not only closed but concealed.

Guided by instinct, it weaves a circular web, rather less than the diameter of the burrow, and works into it a quantity of earth. A second and rather larger web is placed upon it, similarly mixed with earth. This process s repeated until the spider has constructed a circular plate of alternate layers of web and earth, nearly twice the thickness of a penny and slightly conical. Eight or ten layers are employed in the manufacture of the plate.

A small portion of this plate is attached to the lining

TRAP-DOOR SPIDER.

of the burrow, the webs, indeed, of the plate being woven into those of the lining, and being a continuation of them. The plate, therefore, forms a door with a silken hinge, and so accurately is it constructed, that when it is closed the upper surface is exactly level with the ground.

The spider takes care to cover the upper surface with earth exactly resembling the soil in which the burrow is sunk, even imitating the irregularity and roughness with astonishing fidelity, and fixing lichens on it just as the chaffinch does on its nest. So perfectly is this done that to discover a closed trap-door is almost impossible.

Even when the eye has been directed to the exact spot, it is not easy to find the door. If, however, it be found, and an attempt be made to open it, a tolerably strong resistance will be experienced. This is caused by the inhabitant, which holds firmly with its forelegs to the door and its hind legs to the lining of its web, and resists as long as it can.

So firmly does it retain its hold, that when the nest has been pulled out of the soil and torn asunder, the spider has come away with the upper portion, still holding the door against its foe.

I have already mentioned that the spider always chooses a sloping surface for its burrow. The hinge is invariably placed upon the highest point, so that when the door is opened and the spider issues forth, the door is self-acting and shuts by its own weight.

In the British Museum there is a remarkable example of a burrow with two trap-doors, one in the usual place at the entrance, and the other an inch or two below it.

The reason for this duplicate door was easily discovered. The nest had been made in cultivated ground. Earth had been thrown over the mouth of the burrow and buried it. The inmate had, therefore, burrowed upwards until it had made its way into the open air, and had then constructed a second door.

The most curious example of a trap-door nest that I ever saw was sent to me from India by an officer.

It was made in a mass of clay in the fluting of a pillar, and was discovered quite accidentally. The officer caught sight of a curiously formed stone, and lifting it up was surprised to find it pulled smartly back. On lifting it up again he saw that the supposed stone was a circular door with a silken hinge, and that it formed a cover to a hole in the clay. Seeing a large spider dart into the hole he began to dig out the nest, when the spider again made its appearance, shut the door, and retained its hold so tenaciously that it came away with its nest and was captured.

There are many species of Trap-door spiders, the best known of which is a native of Jamaica, and is scientifically termed *Cteniza nidulans*.

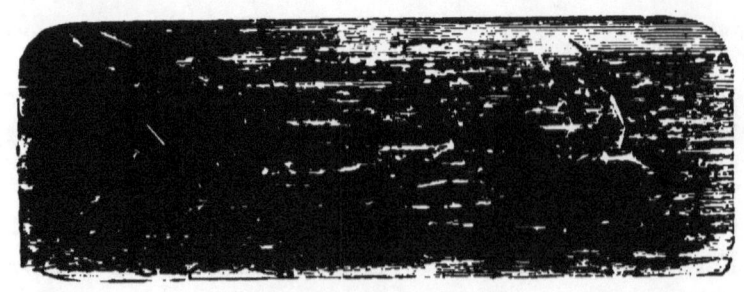

ABOUT SPIDERS AND THEIR WEBS.

CHAPTER IV.

WATER SPIDERS.

WE have already seen that there are spiders who pass the greater part of their lives in the ground, and we now come to a most remarkable group, which live almost entirely under water. I believe that they are never found in salt water, but they are tolerably common in most ditches and streamlets, provided the current be not a strong one.

That spiders should live under water is the more remarkable because they breathe atmospheric air, and might reasonably be expected to die after a long submersion. So they would but for a curious provision of nature, which permits them to store below the surface a sufficient amount of air for respiration.

WATER SPIDERS.

If seen on land there is nothing about the creature to attract attention. It is not larger than a fair-sized garden spider, though its legs are rather long in proportion to its body, and the colour is dark blackish brown. Both the abdomen and legs are thickly coated with hairs, but with this exception there is nothing in its external character to denote the life which it is intended to lead.

These apparently insignificant hairs, however, enable the spider to supply itself with air, and the mode in which it does so is very remarkable.

The creature goes to the surface of the water and moves all its legs very busily, just as if it were trying to crawl out of the water. Suddenly it gives a sharp jerk, or kick, and dives below the surface. It then looks exactly as if it were surrounded by a case of polished silver, owing to a bubble of air which it has enclosed between its long hind legs. On account of this silvery aspect the Water spider is called scientifically *Argyroneta aquatica*, *i.e.* Aquatic Silver-spinner.

Besides the large bubble of the hind legs, there are a number of smaller bubbles which cling to the other legs, and which can be added to the principal bubble when needed. This supply of air is sufficient to last the spider for a considerable time; but there comes a period when it will have to furnish air for others besides itself.

The best plan of watching the proceedings of the Water spider is to place it in a glass vessel, taking care that the glass be of good quality and the vessel not very wide. Some aquatic plants should be also placed in the vessel, the common *Eudorea* being an excellent one for the purpose, as it requires no root. All that is needed is to tie a stone to the end of the plant and let it sink. The *Eudorea* will at first seem languid, as if about to die, but will soon put forth an abundance of fresh shoots, which will choke the vessel unless they are thinned.

If the spiders be in good health they will clamber among the plants, rise to the surface, and dive again. But they will never attempt to escape from the vessel, and so there is no necessity for a cover.

After they have occupied the vessel for a little time, each will seem to take a fancy to a particular spot, always returning to it after rising to the surface. If that spot be examined with a magnifying-glass, a number of threads will be seen between the leaves and stems of the plants, crossing and recrossing each other repeatedly.

When it has spun a considerable number of these threads, the spider gathers its limbs nearly close to the body and moves them as if combing itself. After keeping up this movement for some little time, it gives a smart jerk, and kicks off the bubble of air which surrounds its body. The bubble rises, but is entangled among the silken threads, while the spider goes off to the surface for a fresh supply of air.

Sometimes it seems dissatisfied with its work, turns round, and with another jerk kicks the bubble back again. This I have seen it do several times in succession.

During the earlier part of the year the Water spider makes many of these temporary reservoirs, but when the time comes for egg-laying she sets herself earnestly to work.

Using the threads already mentioned as a sort of scaffolding, she spins among them a silken cocoon about as large as an acorn, and very much of the same shape. The mouth of this cell is always downwards, and is left open. As the spider proceeds with her work, she continues to bring it into the cocoon, so that before long she has made a sub-aquatic habitation exactly on the principle of the diving-bell.

She then takes up her abode within the cell, and fixes about a hundred spherical eggs upon the roof, if we may so call it, covering them with a layer of web, so as to make a separate, saucer-shaped cocoon within the dwelling. Here the young spiders are hatched, and, as is usual with the whole tribe of spiders, the mother waits upon her young and takes care of them until they can go into the water and shift for themselves.

It is as well to supply captive Water spiders with flies or similar food, as, although all spiders can endure a marvellously long fast, they cannot display their power to the best advantage unless they are well fed.

SOME NOXIOUS INSECTS.

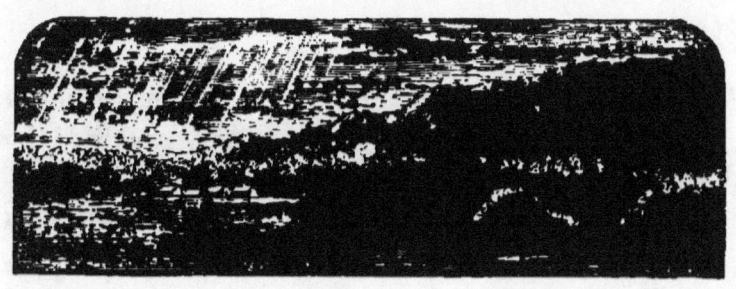

SOME NOXIOUS INSECTS.

CHAPTER I.

INJURIOUS TO MAN.

NOXIOUS insects may be briefly defined as those insects which injure man. Obviously they may do this in two ways. Either they inflict direct injuries on his person, or they indirectly injure him by damaging his property. In either case, they are the result of civilisation.

To the genuine savage no insects are noxious, not even those bloodthirsty parasites which we call by the general name of "vermin." A savage cares nothing for vermin of any kind, and it is not until man is far removed from savages that he begins to object to their presence.

One African traveller, for example—I think the late

Mr. J. Baines—was hospitably entertained in the hut of a Kafir chief. During the night he was awakened by the most intolerable pricking sensations all over his body. On starting up he found that his host, with the kindest intentions, had spread his own kaross, or fur cloak, over his guest. The kaross was swarming with vermin, and they had taken full advantage of their good fortune in finding such a victim. He was obliged to go out of the hut into the open air, and clear himself and his clothes of his tormentors, before he could hope for rest. Yet the owner of the kaross could have felt no inconvenience from them, or he would not have transferred them to his guest.

A curiously similar incident is recorded in the "Arabian Nights" (Lane's edition).

In the story of Noureddin and the Fair Persian, the Caliph is represented as meeting a fisherman, and exchanging clothes with him for the purpose of disguising himself the more effectually. Scarcely had the change been effected than the Caliph felt himself bitten in all quarters, and cried out with pain. The fisherman, accustomed from childhood to consider the presence of vermin as a necessary adjunct of existence, simply advises the Caliph to take no notice of them, but to allow them to go on biting until he was accustomed to them, and he would feel them no longer.

Clean skins and clothing are inconsistent with vermin; and, indeed, a theory has not been wanting that the parasites in question are directly beneficial to the non-washing races of mankind, by serving as a succedaneum for soap and water, and, by the irritation which they cause, keeping up a healthy action of the skin.

LOCUST.

As to secondarily noxious insects, a savage has no conception of them. He does not till the earth, and consequently has no crops to be devoured. He possesses neither flocks nor herds, and therefore even such insects as the tzetze-fly and gad-fly have no terrors for him.

Take, for example, the most noxious insect which an agriculturist fears, namely, the locust, and see how it affects a savage, say a Bosjesman.

To the South African farmer the locust is the most fearful of pests. A swarm of locusts will mean absolute

MIGRATORY LOCUST.

ruin, for the creatures will destroy in a single night the harvest on which the owner depends for subsistence.

But to the Bosjesman the locust-swarm is an unmixed blessing. He has no crop that the insects can destroy, but he finds in the locust-swarm an abundant store of food without the trouble of hunting for it. He hails the approach of the distant swarm, and as long as it remains in his neighbourhood he enjoys to the full the chief luxury of savage life, *i.e.* eating to repletion day after day, and only sleeping off the effects of one meal to begin another.

Take, again, the great Palm Weevil (*Calandra palmarum*), the huge jaws of which are so destructive to the palm-trees, and so noxious to the cultivator.

The savage exults when he sees the traces of the "gru-gru," as this larva is called, for it forms one of his

PALM, OR GRU-GRU, WEEVIL.

most dainty articles of food, and all the more valuable because it requires no cooking. The gru-gru is simply cut out of the tree, held by the head, and eaten alive, as we eat oysters in this country. Many a savage, and white man also, when leading a savage life, has been indebted for his very existence to the Palm Weevil. To the cultivator of the palm this weevil is one of the worst of noxious insects. To the same man, when travelling out of the reach of civilisation, it is a priceless boon.

Then there are the various Termites, the terror of civilised man, the destroyers of his furniture, books, and papers, the devourers of every piece of woodwork in his house, and sometimes the underminers of the house itself.

The savage values them for the various ways in which they contribute towards his livelihood.

NESTS OF WHITE ANT, OR TERMITES.

In the first place he eats them.

In this country we revolt at the idea of eating insects, but in savage lands the Termite is eaten, not as a matter of absolute necessity, but of choice. Indeed, a savage king, to whom a traveller presented some apricot jam, declared it to be the best food he knew next to Termites.

Then, the nests which these insects rear are of great service to the savage. There are several animals, popularly called Ant Bears, which feed chiefly on the Termites, or White Ants, as they are wrongly called. These creatures are furnished with enormous claws, with which they tear out the whole interior of the nest, leaving nothing but the shell of clay, baked as hard as a brick in the sunbeams.

Such empty nests serve several purposes. In the first place they are utilised as ovens, in which the native hunters can cook the animals killed by them.

Then, such savages as build huts find that nothing makes so good a floor for their houses as Termites nests ground into a powder mixed with water, beaten down until quite smooth and level, and left to harden in the rays of the tropical sun.

Lastly, they serve as tombs for the dead. The corpse is thrust into the empty nest through the hole left by the Ant Bear, the aperture is closed with stones and thorns, and there the body may remain undisturbed by any foe except man.

The common Water-Boatman insects, which are shaped so much like boats, swim on their keel-shaped backs, and use their long hind legs as oars. All of them possess sharp, strong beaks, capable of penetrating the human skin, and depositing in the wound a poisonous secretion, which causes a dull, throbbing pain lasting for several hours.

There are many species of Water-Boatmen, but those which belong to the genus *Corixa*, and can be known by the flattened ends of their bodies, have the sharpest beaks, the most virulent poison, and consequently are the most noxious when handled. Even in England these Corixæ are apt to be rather unpleasant insects, but there are some parts of Mexico where the lakes swarm with Corixæ of very much larger dimensions than any British species.

Yet these insects, noxious as we might think them, are very useful to the comparatively uncivilised natives, who eat, not the Corixæ, but their eggs.

At the proper time of the year the natives sink large bundles of reeds in the water. In a week or two the reeds are thickly covered with Corixa eggs, which are scraped off and the reeds returned to the water. In fact, the Corixa is treated very much like the mussel in the French breeding beds. The eggs, after being scraped off, are pressed into cakes, which are cooked and used for consumption, under the name of "haoutle."

Even the dread mosquito, the only insect which a savage can have an excuse for ranking as noxious, is really of direct value to some savage tribes.

Livingstone mentions that the shores of the Lake Nyassa swarm with mosquitos. The late Mr. Baines told me that no one who has not seen the mosquito swarm that hang on the banks of these African lakes, can form even a conception of their multitude. They fill the air so that they seem to be an almost solid mass. If a lamp be lighted, they put it out by settling on it, while the hum of their wings is almost like the roaring of the sea in the ears of a diver.

Yet the natives can utilise even these terrible pests, which are so venomous that not even a mule could stray on the banks of the lake and live through the night. But the mosquito never seems to travel to any great distance from the water in which it passed through its previous stages of existence, and the natives can avoid it by sleeping in spots far removed from the water's edge.

They do more than this; they sweep the mosquitos into large bags, press them together and form them into cakes, just as is done with the eggs of the Corixa. These cakes go by the name of "kungo." They are circular, about eight inches in diameter, and an inch or so in thickness. When eaten they are said to bear some resemblance to caviare in flavour.

Before quitting this part of the subject, we must not lose sight of the fact that none of the so-called noxious insects, even though they cause direct annoyance to man, were created for that purpose. Take, for example, the mosquito swarms above mentioned. Man is not the normal food of the mosquito, which can and does maintain existence without ever seeing a human being. But when man presents himself in the tract already inhabited by the mosquitos, he becomes an intruder and has to suffer the penalty of his intrusion.

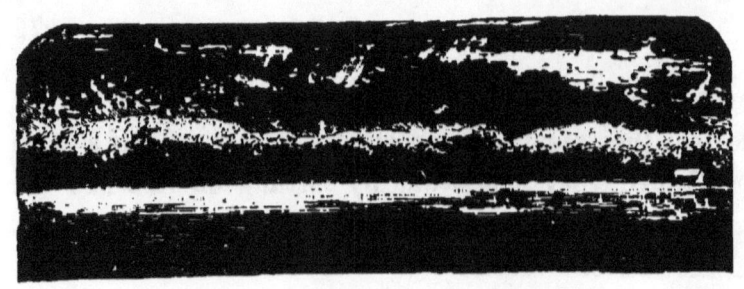

SOME NOXIOUS INSECTS.

CHAPTER II.

WOOL AND WOOD DESTROYERS.

THE clothes moths, it is easy to understand, can do no harm to the naked savage, but it is not so easy to comprehend that they can be of any benefit to civilised man. Yet the whole tribe of clothes moths are of inestimable service to mankind, whether naked savage or broadcloth-wearing Europeans.

Let it be remembered that so long as woollen clothes are in use the moth never touches them; but if stored away in treasuries and not put to use by man, the moth comes and uses them for itself. Man does his best—or worst—to waste the gifts of God, but He who made both the recipient and the gift abhors waste, and fixes limits to man's power of wasting.

WOOL AND WOOD DESTROYERS. 277

Where is all the wool that sheep have furnished since

sheep were created? Every year it is removed from the

sheep, either artificially by man, or in the ordinary course of nature, just as birds moult their plumage. Now hair is all but imperishable, as may be seen in the Egyptian wig in the British Museum. Three thousand years have passed since it was shorn, and yet it is as bright and glossy as when it left the hands of the maker. If the wool had been suffered to remain untouched, it would have remained until the present day and choked up the face of the habitable earth. But whether used by man or not, it has still been used, and has returned to the earth whence it came.

Even in our own country it is interesting to trace the return of the wool to its parent earth.

The greater part is used by man as clothing. If he cease to use it, the clothes moths, museum beetles, and their kin attack it, and before long have devoured it, so that it again returns to earth.

Some of it is torn off by brambles and left hanging to the prickles; but it is not wasted. The little birds carry it off and use it for their nests as long as it is capable of acting as a warm, soft bed for the eggs and young. Afterwards, when the birds have left it, the moths and beetles come to it and devour it, just as they devour woollen clothes. If they did not do so the branches of every tree would be so clogged with nests that the leaves could not grow and the tree would perish.

In this country we are but little plagued with the wood-eating insects. Their numbers are few and their size insignificant. Within doors we suffer but little from them, and even at the worst, old furniture can only become "worm-eaten." The little holes with which we are so familiar in old chairs and chests are the openings of tiny galleries which perforate the wood, and by which the insect that has caused them has escaped, after passing through its stages of egg, grub, and pupa.

Several insects—all being beetles—make these tunnels,

SCOLYTUS DESTRUCTOR TUNNELS.

and the principal of them is called *Anobium tesselatum*. Popularly it is known as the "Death-watch," because, in common with several other insects, the male calls to its mate by knocking its head against the wood, and producing a sound bearing some resemblance to the ticking of a watch.

Out of doors there are but few wood-eating insects, and with one or two exceptions they are not supposed to do much harm in this country.

One of these exceptions is the *Scolytus destructor*, an insect which infests trees, especially the elm, and makes multitudinous tunnels between the wood and the bark, often separating the latter from the tree and causing it to fall in large sheets to the ground. The tree, as a

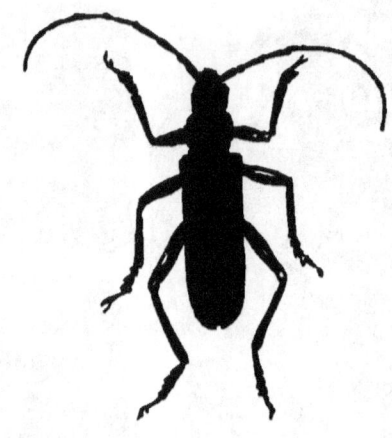

MUSK BEETLE.

matter of course, dies, and, equally as a matter of course, the Scolytus is looked upon as its destroyer.

Entomologists of the present day, however, are scarcely disposed to take this view of the case, and consider that the Scolytus does not attack sound and healthy trees, but only those which are dying.

Besides the Scolytus, there are very few other wood-devouring beetles sufficiently known to possess popular names. The Musk Beetle, conspicuous as it is for size of body, splendour of colour, and sweetness of scent, is curiously little known; while, except to entomologists, the *Ptilinus*, the *Sinodendron*, the *Clytus*, and *Rhagium*, are not known at all.

The larva of the Stag Beetle feeds upon the roots of trees, and those which are attacked by it may mostly be known by the dead branches at the top. But it is pro-

GOAT-MOTH CATERPILLAR.

bable that the tree had begun to die before it was attacked, and that the presence of the beetle larva was the consequence and not the cause of the tree's death.

Then there is the caterpillar of the Goat Moth, which feeds chiefly on old willow-trees, and riddles them with its burrows, which in some places are large enough to admit a man's finger. Here again, however, the tree is probably in a dying state before it is attacked by the moth.

In the hotter parts of the world, however, the wood-devouring insects are more than mere annoyances in houses, the most dreaded of them all being the Termites or White Ants. They will devour every piece of woodwork in the house. They find their way into beams, and eat the whole of the wood, with the exception of a shell scarcely thicker than the paper on which this narrative is printed.

They will attack a table, eating their way through the

GREAT TERMITE.

floor into the legs, and hollowing it so that on leaning upon the table, apparently sound as it is, it breaks down and crumbles into a heap of dusty fragments. They have even been known to get into a garden and hollow out the peasticks, so that the first wind blew them down together with their burden. If they find their way into boxes in which papers are kept, they will devour almost the whole of every bundle, leaving nothing but the uppermost sheet and the edges of the others.

So in the dwellings of civilised man they are an unmitigated pest. But it must be remembered that house-beams, furniture, and documents are not the normal food of the Termites, which existed for ages before man built houses, made furniture, or penned documents.

Remove man from the scene, and how will the Termites be affected? Not at all; for they are found to be flourishing in places where man has never intruded himself. Their chief object is to co-operate with other creatures in preserving the balance of creation, of restoring to earth that which sprang from it, and so to enable earth to reproduce new forms of life.

Remove the Termites and the wood-destroying creatures from the scene, and there would not be a forest left in the world. Annihilate them all, and see what would happen. When a tree died, it would be blown down, fall, and lie there as long as the world lasts. It would cumber the ground so that no new tree could take its place, and so, in the course of a couple of thousand years or so, instead of a forest, there would be a tangled mass of dead, dry trunks and branches, through which no new growths could force their way.

Then the abolition of the foliage would alter the climate, and produce a perpetual drought, so that even if grass and herbage tried to grow, they would be withered up for want of water. It would be a pathless wilderness —a Sahara of wood instead of sand.

But see what happens when the wood-eating insects come into operation.

As long as a tree is healthy and vigorous they do not touch it; but in the course of nature its term of existence is fulfilled, and it dies. Simultaneously it is attacked by hosts of wood-eating insects, which bore their way into it, lay their eggs, and so establish within it a series of rapidly increasing colonies which weaken its substance. At the first tempest down it comes. Then comes the rain, and penetrates into the wood through the tunnels made by the insects. Fungi now are formed, and still further weaken the wood, making it soft and fit for the food of another set of devourers.

Waterton in his "Wanderings," details most graphically this portion of insect work :—"Step a few paces aside, and cast thine eye on that remnant of a Mora. Best part of its branches, once so high and ornamental, now lie on the ground in sad confusion, one upon the other, all shattered and fungus-grown, and a prey to millions of insects, which are employed in destroying them.

"Put thy foot on that large trunk thou seest to the left. It seems entire amid the surrounding fragments. Mere outward appearance, delusive phantom of what it once was! Tread on it, and, like the fuss-ball, it will break into dust."

What happens next is evident enough. It sinks into the ground and is incorporated with it, thus making room for a new tree to spring up in its stead, and supplying to the ground the elements necessary for the nutriment of the fresh growth. Thus it is that, were it not for the Noxious Insects, man would long have ceased to maintain his place in the world.

SOME NOXIOUS INSECTS.

CHAPTER III.

OUR BENEFACTORS.

IN the uncivilised days of England the carrot, the turnip, the asparagus, the cabbage, the celery, and other garden plants, were mere weeds, and, in consequence, the insects which fed upon them were unheeded by man. Our semi-savage predecessors could find no fault with the cabbage caterpillars, with the turnip grub, the celery fly, or the asparagus beetle, simply because the plants on which they fed had not been brought into cultivation, and their destroyers could not be ranked among noxious insects.

So at the present day we do not cultivate the stinging nettle, ranking it among the weeds, and, in consequence, we rather look upon the insects which feed upon it as our benefactors. But if some clever gardener were to develop the stinging nettle into a garden vegetable, the beautiful Tortoiseshell, Atalanta, and Peacock butterflies would be placed among our noxious insects, inasmuch as their larvæ feed upon the plant. Perhaps

BUTTERFLIES.

the gardeners of Dreepdailie, who, according to Andrew Fairservice, cultivated that vegetable under forcing glasses, held precisely the same opinion of the insects.

There are several insects to which all civilised nations confess themselves indebted. The bee, for example,

SILKWORMS.

furnishes us with honey and wax, and so we praise it for its industry, though we have no word of commendation for the common wasp, which is quite as industrious and unselfish as the bee, or the sand wasp, which works infinitely harder.

The silkworms are almost venerated, because we use the silk which they produce. Yet there is not a caterpillar, either of butterfly or moth, that does not produce silk of some kind.

The cochineal insect is almost as important to man as the silkworm, and, tiny as it is, it furnishes the means of existence to thousands of human beings. Two of its near relatives are also of exceeding value, one furnishing a wax equal in many respects to that of the bee, and the other producing the "lac" so invaluable for lacquer work, sealing-wax, and varnish.

Yet, were it not that we have learned the value of their counterbalancing qualities, every one of these creatures would be justifiably ranked among the noxious insects.

Take the bee. A child, who is ignorant of the character of the bee, seizes it, is stung, and has very good reason for considering it as a very noxious insect.

Afterwards, when he learns that the bee furnishes the sweet honey which tickles his palate, he pardons the sting which has hurt his hand. He has learned one of the counterbalancing qualities of a noxious insect. As he increases in knowledge and civilisation, he learns that the wax, which as a child he would have flung aside after draining it of the honey, is by far the more valuable product of the two, and that some of the arts—metal statuary, for example—could not be conducted without it.

Take the silkworm. It destroys the leaves of the mulberry-tree, and injures the crop of fruit which man wants for himself, so that, to a race of men sufficiently civilised to cultivate the mulberry-tree, it would be classed among the noxious insects.

But further knowledge about the habits of the creature enables mankind to understand its counterbalancing qualities, and so, although the silkworm consumes far more mulberry foliage than it did when it was considered merely as a noxious insect, we have learned to compare the value of the silk which it produces with that of the leaves which it devours, and prize the silkworm as a source of national wealth.

In these few instances the counterbalancing qualities are so directly beneficial to civilised man as to be obvious even to the most unobservant among us. Semi-civilised man finds similar direct benefits in various insects. For example, in many countries the social wasps are almost as valuable as the social bees, the grubs of both being a highly-prized article of food.

In Mexico there are most remarkable ants, popularly called Hormigas miêleras, and scientifically known as *Myrmecocystus Mexicanus*. These ants are most wonderful beings, for they not only collect honey, but store it for future use in vessels so strange that their existence would almost be thought impossible.

The Honey Ant makes its store vessels from the bodies of the workers.

First, it bites the end of the abdomen, thereby setting up an inflammation, which closes the apertures of the body. Then it feeds the maimed creature with honey, pouring it into the mouth of the living honey-pot just as the bee pours honey into its crop. This process is continually repeated until the body of the store ant is dis-

HONEY ANT.

tended to an astonishing size with honey, the skin being stretched to such an extent that it is sufficiently transparent to show the honey within.

It cannot escape, for its body is so heavy that the limbs are insufficient to carry it, and so it remains in the nest until the honey is wanted. In Mexico these ants are so plentiful that they form regular articles of commerce, being sold by measure in the markets, and used for the purpose of making mead. Specimens may be seen in the British Museum.

Were it not for this property the Honey Ant would be one of the many insects which are called noxious. But its counterbalancing qualities are such that, in its own country, it almost equals the honey bee in its value to man.

Even in Europe the ants are not without their direct use to man. Every one knows the common Wood Ant (*Formica rufa*), sometimes called the Horse Ant, which heaps up fragments of dried grass, broken twigs, dead leaves, and similar objects, into large hills. If one of these hills be opened a curiously pungent odour will be perceived, not unlike that of green wood when heated in the fire. If the face or even the hand be held in the hollow of the nest a sharp, pricking sensation will be felt, as if the skin were pricked with thousands of tiny needles.

This is caused by a peculiar secretion of the Ant, called "formic acid," from its origin.

I have seen a dog, who had inadvertently scratched a hole in one of these nests, suffer terribly from his indiscretion. He was half mad with pain and terror, and half blinded by the formic acid which had found its way into his eyes, besides irritating his nostrils, as if pepper had been thrown into them.

In England the use of this acid is not recognised, and the ants are considered simply as noxious insects, on account of the pain which they can cause when they attack human beings. In Norway, and Sweden, however, the Wood Ants are highly valued, as a peculiar vinegar, flavoured with the formic acid, is prepared from them. A jar of ant vinegar often forms part of a present to a bride on her wedding-day.

DRAGON-FLIES.

DRAGON-FLIES.

CHAPTER I.

THEIR LIFE HISTORY.

NEVER was a more appropriate name than that of Dragon-fly, which has been applied to a well-known group of insects. Like the dragons of fable, the dragon-flies are ever voracious, powerful, strong-jawed, fierce, and swifter in air than on land. But the dragon-flies are even more terrible than the dragons, for they have been dragons of the water as well as of land, and pursued their prey beneath the waves as swiftly as through the air. There are many destructive creatures in the world which feed upon living prey, but there are none which are more voracious or destructive than the dragon-flies.

The life of a dragon-fly may be divided into two unequal parts, the longer portion of its existence being spent in the water, and the shorter portion on land. Whether it be aquatic or terrestrial, it is equally ferocious, and, as we shall see, is equally fitted for the purpose of preying upon other creatures.

The eggs of this insect are dropped into the water by the parent, and are there hatched. The little creature grows with great rapidity, and, for convenience' sake, we will pass over the first few months of its life, until it reaches the length of an inch and a half, or thereabouts, when it will assume the form shown in the lower figure of the accompanying illustration.

It is of a pale greyish-brown colour, with a few darker spots and bars; and when taken out of the water, only struggles vaguely in its attempts to escape, without giving the least indication of its wonderful structure and singular habits.

There is no difficulty in taking these creatures, which abound in almost every pond, and can be captured by scraping the water weeds with an ordinary insect net.

The best plan of watching them is to take a single specimen and place it in a shallow basin of water, which should not be more than two inches deep. Scatter a little sand in the water, so that it shall lie smoothly on the bottom of the basin. There will be no need to cover the basin, for the creature will not endeavour to leave the water.

It will crawl very feebly and slowly for a time, but presently it will glide through the water without any apparent means of propulsion. Look at the sand, and

THE DRAGON-FLY; ITS THREE STAGES.

you will find that whenever the insect glides along in this mysterious manner, the sand is scooped away so as to form a shallow groove.

This is caused by the singular mode of propulsion employed by the dragon-fly while still in the larval state.

DRAGON-FLY LARVA TAKING ITS PREY.

If you look at the tail of the insect, you will see that there are three radiating spikes. These surround the entrance to a tube which traverses nearly the whole body of the insect. By a peculiar structure, water can be drawn gently into the tube, and expelled with greater or less violence, thus driving the insect forward exactly on the principle of the rocket.

Were it not for this wonderful organism, the insect would not catch the active aquatic creatures on which it feeds, and could not carry on its mission of destruction. Perhaps the reader may have visited an aquarium, and seen an octopus in motion. Like the dragon-fly larva, it crawls slowly and almost uncertainly, but, like the same larva, it can shoot through the water with considerable speed to a definite point, propelled by similar machinery, and engaged on a similar errand.

They are cannibals to a certain extent. They will not attack each other by preference, as long as any other prey can be found, but they cannot endure hunger, and in default of legitimate prey, will attack and devour their own kind. In fact, if they are to be reared in captivity, each must have a vessel to itself. Put two into the same vessel, and in a few hours they will have fought, and the victor will have begun to eat the vanquished.

I have noticed that they are always on the look-out for insects which fall into the water. I had often wondered why it was that flies, moths, &c., disappeared almost as soon as they began to struggle, and it was not until I had seen my own specimens seize their prey that I found the key to the mystery.

They came gliding up from below, not moving a limb, grasped their victim and sank again, their grey bodies being curiously indistinguishable in the water, especially when broken lights and shadows are thrown upon its surface. Moreover, owing to the structure of the remarkable organ which they use when seizing their prey, they do' not come close to the surface, but can remain well below it, as shown in the illustration.

Owing to the structure of the breathing apparatus, the dragon-fly larva can no more breathe out of the water than we can breathe in it; and consequently it is never to be seen on land. As a rule, the other insects on which it mostly feeds are also inhabitants of the water, as is the case with the May-fly larva, which is represented as being seized.

DRAGON-FLIES.

CHAPTER II.

THEIR APPALLING VORACITY.

THE mouths of insects are most complicated organs, comprising different sets of jaws, lips, and various appendages. They are modified to suit the task which they have to perform, and though the strong jaws and mouth-brush of the stag-beetle, the slender spiral proboscis of the butterfly, and the venom-bearing weapon of the gnat or flea appear to be utterly distinct from each other, they are really modifications of the same organs.

In the dragon-fly larva, these organs are modified in a most astonishing manner. If the reader will refer to page 299 he will see that the smaller insect is being grasped between two curved jaws, the bases of which are jointed to the corners of a flattened and somewhat triangularly-shaped horny plate. When these jaws are closed, they lie so closely against the edge of the horny plate that they can hardly be distinguished from it.

The triangular plate is jointed below to a narrow plate about equal to it in length, and that again is jointed to the lower portion of the mouth.

In the illustration, this apparatus is shown as it appears when extended. When closed it is folded under the head, and is not visible from above. It is known to entomologists by the popular name of "mask," because the front of the head is hidden by it as if concealed by a mask. Its appearance when folded may be seen by reference to page 304.

As soon as the dragon-fly larva has seized its prey, it folds the mask, and by that action brings the victim close to its mouth, so that it can be eaten without having a chance of escape.

If the reader will examine a crab, lobster, or shrimp before eating it, and will fold the joints of its claws, he will find that the claws exactly coincide with the entrance of the mouth, and just the same structure is found in the larva of the dragon-fly.

The perfect insect does not need the mask, for its movements through the air are so rapid, and its wings so powerful, that no other insect can escape when once the dragon-fly gives chase

Unlike the moths and butterflies, whose change from the larval to the pupal state is so strongly marked in the caterpillar and chrysalis, the pupa of the dragon-fly differs little externally from that of the larva, except that the two projections on the back which conceal the future wings are larger and more distinct.

It is as voracious as ever, but towards the middle of

Water line.

THE DRAGON-FLY BEING RELEASED.

summer it becomes more languid in its movements, cares less and less for food, and at last ceases to eat altogether.

Meanwhile, a wonderful change has been taking place in its breathing apparatus—its gills fail to extract oxygen from the water, and it feels that it must breathe air or die. It makes its way to any object which projects out of the water, preferring a reed or sedge if it can be found.

Slowly it crawls upwards, for its legs are quickly stiffening, and at last it reaches a suitable height above the water; here it stops and awaits its escape from bondage.

The skin rapidly dries when out of the water, the insect struggles for breath, and in its struggles the dry skin is split along the back, and for the first time in its life the dragon-fly breathes the air for which it has longed.

New strength comes with every respiration, and before very long, the insect can extend the rent in the skin and draw out its head. Presently, the legs are drawn from their former coverings like swords from their scabbards, the feet are used as they are freed, and soon the whole upper part of the dragon-fly is released.

The wings, which are as yet nothing but thick, soft, and apparently solid masses, are freed from their coverings, and by degrees the whole insect is withdrawn from the empty shell, which is left clinging with its hollow and now transparent legs to the plant up which the pupa had climbed.

If possible, the dragon-fly will find a foot-hold on a neighbouring stem or leaf, and will then be able to extricate itself more quickly. But, if it can find none, it simply allows itself to bend backwards, as shown in the illustration, until it can cling to the stem. The last segment of the abdomen is then drawn out of the aperture, and the insect is finally released.

The empty skin is not in the least injured except by the rent in the back. The jointed mask still remains in its place, together with its jaws. The eyes seem still to

THE DRAGON-FLY.

be there, and the feet retain their hold so firmly, that if the cast skin be wanted as a specimen, the plant can be cut off, dried, and together with the clinging skin placed in a suitable case.

When thus released, the dragon-fly is at first helpless, and its wings give no promise of their future beauty.

They are, however, permeated with air-tubes, and at every respiration the air is forced into them, so as gradually and slowly to loosen the many folds in which they had been packed. By degrees a tremulous motion shows itself, and the wings begin to show like sails unfurled.

After a period varying according to the warmth and dryness of the day, the wings are opened to their full extent, and the dragon-fly darts off, to be as fierce and voracious in the air as it had been in the water.

Its power of wing is marvellous. There is a well-known anecdote of a swallow chasing a dragon-fly into a greenhouse, and vainly endeavouring to catch it, in spite of the confined space which prohibited the full use of its wings.

Its voracity is almost appalling. A large butterfly, when caught, is gone directly. The dragon-fly crumples up the body of its victim in its powerful jaws, and, though the wings are generally allowed to fall, a part of them will often follow the body and disappear in the dragon-fly's insatiable maw.

A lion cannot compare with a dragon-fly in point of voracity. Suppose that any one were to assert that a lion had eaten twenty or thirty large ducks, and four or five geese, without pausing, we should say that he was testing our credulity by relating a feat that no animal could perform.

But, suppose he were to add that the lion, after being cut asunder, did not die, but ate the severed portions of his own body, we should be disposed to set down the narrator as a madman. Yet, this is just what a dragon-fly has done, flies being substituted for fowls and large garden spiders for geese. The insect, when accidentally struck asunder, really has been known to eat the whole of its own abdomen when presented to it, and any other dragon-fly would probably act in a similar manner.

This fierce and active terrestrial life is not a long one, and may be measured by weeks rather than months. It depends upon the supply of food, and when insects begin to fail in numbers as the season becomes colder, the dragon-fly can live no longer. Drawn by a fresh instinct, it again seeks the water in which it had so long lived, deposits its eggs, and dies.

THE HORSE AND HIS STRUCTURE.

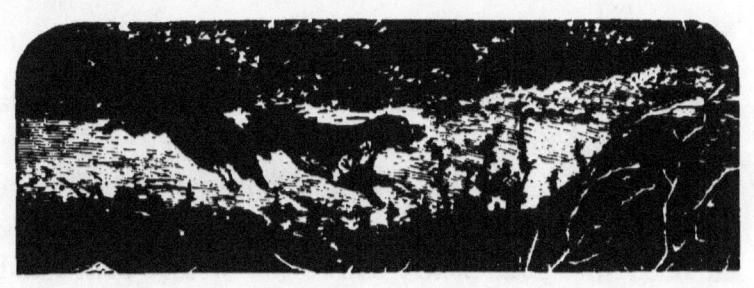

THE HORSE AND HIS STRUCTURE.

CHAPTER I.

THE LEFT OR NEAR FOREFOOT.

LET us take for our study the left or "near" forefoot of the horse.

If the reader will look at the skeleton of a horse he will see that the fore leg is the analogue of the human arm. The so-called "knee" is in fact the wrist, with its eight small bones. The "shank" or "cannon" bone is really the "metacarpal" bone of the middle finger, *i.e.* the bone which, in the hand, runs from the wrist to the root of the finger.

Then comes the "pastern," which is the finger itself, the last or third joint being called the "coffin" or "pedal" bone, which is surrounded by the marvellously complicated structure which we call the hoof. This is identical with the nail on the human finger.

The bones of the thumb and the other fingers are not developed in the horses of the present epoch, being modified into little bones, known as "splint" bones, and invisible until the skin and soft parts are removed. In the earlier days of the world, horses with five toes in-

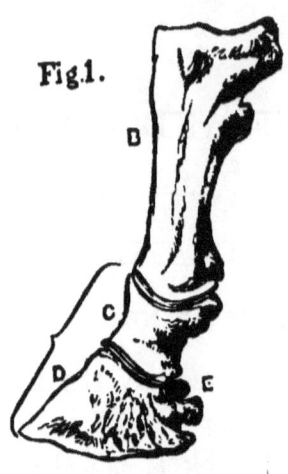

BONES OF PASTERN.

habited the earth, but in successive ages the outer fingers became absorbed, until, at last, the horse walked on two fingers of the fore limbs, and two toes of the hind legs.

In Fig. 1, B represents the first joint of the middle finger, popularly called the long pastern bone; C is the second joint, or short pastern; and D is the coffin, pedal, or distal bone.

These bones do not rest perpendicularly upon each

other, but they form an obtuse angle, so as to give elasticity to the structure.

On looking at the illustration, the reader will see that

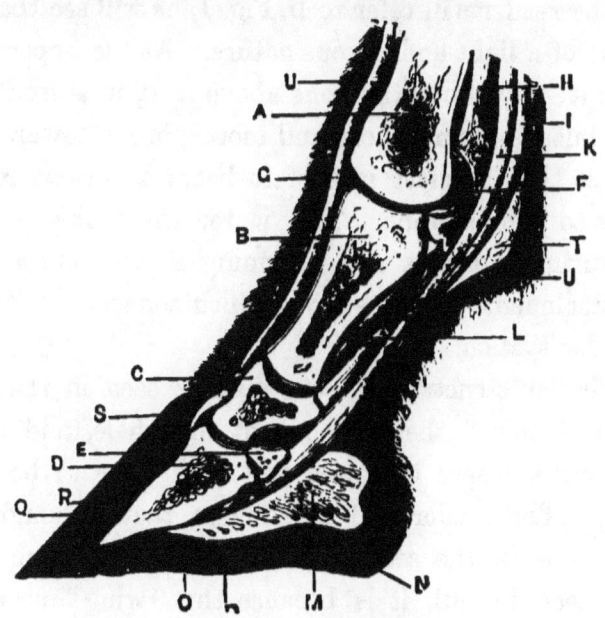

SECTION OF PASTERN.

A, Cannon or Shank Bone.
B, Long Pastern Bone.
C, Short Pastern Bone.
D, Coffin, Pedal, or Distal Bone.
E, Navicular Bone.
F, Sesamoid Bone.
G, Extensor Tendon.
H, Suspensory Ligament.
I } Upper branches of Flexor Ten-
K } don.
L, Upper Branch of Suspensory Ligament.
M, Soft Frog.
N, Hard Frog.
O, Horny Sole.
P, Sensitive Sole.
Q, Vascular Structures.
R, Crust.
S, Coronary Cushion or Secreting Portion.
T, Fatty Cushion.
U, U, Skin.

the centre of the figure is occupied by bone. At A is the lower part of the cannon bone; B is the long pastern bone; c the short pastern; and D the coffin, or last bone of the middle finger. The same letters are employed to designate the same bones in both the illustrations.

If the reader will refer to D, Fig. 1, he will see that the bone is of a light and porous nature. At the upper part, where it plays upon the bone above it, c, it is stout and solid, but it becomes more and more porous towards the edge, so that the last inch of it bears a curious resemblance to pumice-stone. This is for the double purpose of insuring lightness and obtaining a large surface for the attachments of the tendons which connect it with the muscular system.

A similar structure of bone may be seen in the skull of the elephant, the jaw-bone of the whale, and many other cases where lightness and bulk have to be combined. The reader will also notice that although the coffin bone in the section looks unlike the same bone when seen in full, it is because the "wing" near the spectator is cut away, and that the other is hidden behind the soft structures.

In the first place, there are no muscles in the foot. The muscular power is in that part of the leg which lies above the so-called "knee," and the bones are worked by tendons or "ligaments" running from the muscles down the shank or "metacarpus," A, and fastened to the bones of the foot. The human fingers are worked in just the same way. Let the reader grasp his fore arm with one hand, and then clench the other. The swelling of the muscles under the grasp will show where the power resides.

Taking the front of the foot first, and beginning from the bone, we find a sort of cord marked G. This is called the "extensor" ligament, and is fastened to the front of the coffin bone so as to straighten the joint. As comparatively little force has to be exerted by it, the tendon is of no very great size.

Now let us look at the back of the foot, beginning at the bone as before. At H is seen a very stout tendon which serves to suspend the long and short pastern bones, and is therefore called the "suspensory." Passing downwards, it comes over a small, loose, rounded bone, shown in section at F, and then divides into two parts. The first, which is marked L, is fastened to the long pastern bone, B, and the other, which lies just below it, to the short pastern bone, C.

Next to this comes an enormously powerful "flexor" tendon, which is exactly the reverse of the preceding, being single below, and dividing above into two branches, marked I K. At E is the section of a very remarkable accessory bone, which is somewhat analogous to the human knee-cap, or "patella." It is called the shuttle or "navicular" bone, from its shape, which somewhat resembles the outlines of a shuttle or a little boat (*navicula*). Small though it be, it is of extreme importance, inasmuch as bad shoeing causes inflammation, and sets up the terrible navicular disease, from which few horses recover.

The chief object of this bone, which lies between the "wings" of the coffin bone, is to act as a sort of pulley, and afford a better leverage. Passing over this bone, as is seen in the section, the tendon is attached to the sole of the coffin bone, so as to bend the joint when the muscle to which it belongs is contracted.

The projection T, which is so conspicuous in the pastern, is due to a fatty cushion, the object of which is very uncertain.

Now we will take the protective covering of this mechanism, and see how on the exterior it is hard enough to bear the weight of the horse even upon rocky or stony ground, while it is so soft within that it can be furnished with arteries, sinews, and nerves. The horny outside of the hoof is called the "crust" (R in the section), and is so formed that as it is worn away below, under ordinary circumstances, the growth and waste exactly counterbalance each other.

THE HORSE AND HIS STRUCTURE.

CHAPTER II.

THE HOOF, SOLE, ETC.

IF the reader can manage to look at the under surface of a horse's foot that never has been touched by the farrier, he will see that it has the appearance given in illustration (p. 318). It seems to be divided into two parts, the heel portion, looking something like the Broad Arrow of the Government, V, the Y-like barbs of the arrow forming the "bars of the horny frog," while the projecting rounded portions at the ends of the bars are called the "glumes," or heels of the frog. The outline of the edge of the hoof is beautifully rounded, and the "sole" unites it with the frog, the place where the sole and crust join each other being technically known as the White Line, or Commissure.

There is a peculiarity about the sole which needs notice. The fibres of the crust, or wall of the hoof, lie nearly perpendicularly, are supplied with new matter from above, and are worn away by friction below. Those of the sole are not subject to friction. Instead, therefore, of being gradually worn away, the horn is

UNDER SURFACE, UNTOUCHED HOOF.

secreted in flat plates, which flake off successively when their work is done.

Contrast this hoof with the same organ as it appears after the farrier has worked his will on it. The frog was made for the purpose of resting on the ground, and by its great elasticity diminishing the shock caused by the tread of so heavy an animal. So the first thing that a farrier does is to cut away the frog. Mr. Fleming mentions that he has seen a gentleman's coachman stop his horses, get off the box, and cut away the frogs from their feet simply because he thought that they were touching the ground—the very object for which they were made.

Then the farrier assumes that the sole is much too thick, and so pares it away with his drawing-knife until it yields, or "springs," as the technical word is, to the pressure of his thumb-nail. Mr. Fleming states that he

HORSE-HOOF, IMPROVED BY THE FARRIER.

has seen the sole pared as thin as parchment, so that the blood-vessels could be seen through it.

What kind of structure is protected by the sole may be seen by examining the transverse section of the front of the hoof on next page. The drawing was made from a specimen which had just been dissected, and which is now in the College of Surgeons.

At the edge is the hard external horn of the "crust," marked D. Inside it is the sensitive portion, C. At A is shown one of the most remarkable parts of the hoof.

Instead of being a simple horny box, it is formed of thin horny plates, called the horny laminæ, set on their edges side by side, very much like the leaves of a closed fan. The number of these laminæ is about six or seven hundred if counted only upon the crust, but as they return over the interior of the frog their number would be doubled. I mention seven hundred on the authority of several of our best veterinary surgeons, but in all the

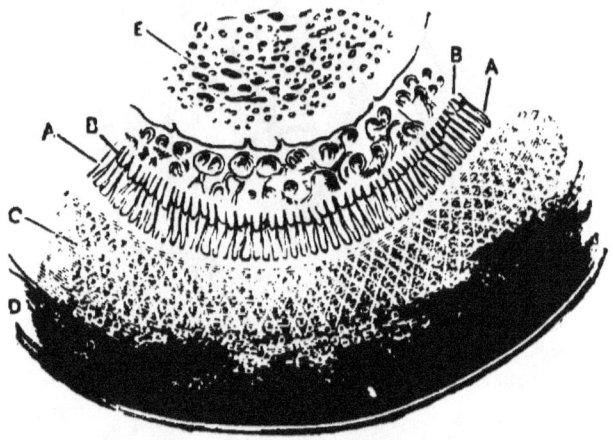

FRONT OF HOOF: TRANSVERSE SECTION.

specimens that I have examined I have found that six hundred is the average.

Between the bone E and the horn is a layer of vascular and sensitive structure, *i.e.* which is traversed by arteries, veins, and nerves. The blood-vessels are rather large near the bone, but become smaller near the horn, where they are formed into vascular laminæ dipping between the laminæ of the horn, and so firmly attached to them that to pull off the hoof in a fresh state is almost impossible.

The beauty of this structure when fresh, both in form and colour, is beyond description, and the illustration, which is little more than a diagram, so as not to confuse the eye with detail, can only represent it as a builder's plan represents a house.

A fair idea of it may be obtained by taking two closed fans, one of scarlet and the other of brown paper. Open them just sufficiently to allow the leaves to interlace, then close them tightly and make a transverse section of them. They will then be seen to give a good idea of this portion of the hoof, the scarlet representing the vascular and the brown the horny laminæ.

This description, however imperfect, will show the reader something of the structures which the untouched hoof protects. The farrier, however, knows absolutely nothing of all these complex mechanisms within the outer hoof. He looks upon the hoof simply as a solid lump of horn without feeling, and so he cuts and carves it to suit the ready-made shoe.

The illustration of a hoof which has passed through the farrier's hands is drawn from a specimen now before me, taken at random from a number of others. The man has cut away the frog because he thinks that the animal will be injured if the frog touches the ground. He has then cut a deep groove at the base of the frog. This is to give a "well-opened heel," as he is pleased to call it.

He has scooped away the sole to "give it spring."

He has scored a deep notch in the toe for the purpose of receiving the "clip" of the shoe. This is evidently a conservative relic of the time when nails were not used, and the shoe attached by three pointed clips hammered over the edge, one in front and one on either side. Then, though this cannot be seen in the illustration, he has improved the whole of the outer surface of the hoof. As this part of the hoof has been furnished with a thin, hard, polished plate, forming a sort of varnish which is impervious to wet, the farrier, as a matter of course, rasps it all away up to the crown. And, as there has been placed round the crown a fringe of hair, which acts as a thatch to the line of junction, and throws off the rain upon the waterproof varnish, he cuts this away with his scissors. Lastly, there having been given to the horny hoof a mottling of soft, and partially translucent, brown, grey-blue, yellow, black, and white, never exactly the same in two hoofs, much less in two horses, the farrier takes a blacking-pot and brush, polishes up the hoofs until they look like patent-leather boots, all four exactly alike, and then contemplates his work with satisfaction. In his own words, he has "turned out a finished job of it."

THE HORSE AND HIS STRUCTURE.

CHAPTER III.

THE SHOE AND THE FROG.

FROM the preceding description of the hoof, the reader will have seen that it is a structure of exceeding complexity, and that if it be considered insufficient for hard work on artificial roads, any appliances for increasing its efficiency ought to interfere as little as possible with its natural condition, and only to be attached by those who understand its structure.

Three of the leading principles of the untouched hoof are—(1) its constant and unequal growth to compensate for friction; (2) its elasticity; and (3) its central bearing.

All these objects are attained by the three kinds of horn which compose the hoof, provided that they are allowed to act without human interference. There is the hard external horn of the crust, formed of flat laminæ set side by side, and admirably suited for clinging to projecting stones when the animal is picking its way over steep or rocky ground. So sure-footed indeed is the animal, that in most places where a man can climb on his hands and knees an unshod horse can follow him. The sure-footedness of the mule is proverbial, and yet there is no appreciable difference in the form and structure of the two creatures. Indeed, the hoof of the ass is formed exactly like that of the horse, and only differs from it in being rather longer and narrower in proportion to its size. Its horny crust is meant to be worn away by constant friction against the hard ground, just as the incisive teeth of the rodents are kept in order by perpetually gnawing hard substances.

The pawing and scraping of the foot, which people are apt to admire as a proof of "blood" or spirit, is owing to the rapid growth of the front portion of the crust. Being protected from friction by the shoe, it grows without hindrance, and so disturbs the balance of the animal, tilting it backwards just as we should be if we removed the thick leather of the boot-heel to the toe. Not knowing that the iron shoe is in the way, the horse tries to scrape down the front of the hoof, so as to bring him to his proper bearings, and is actuated, not by exuberance of spirits, but by uneasiness of foot.

Then comes the sole, serving to protect the sensitive interior of the hoof from the loose and sharp stones, and falling off in successive flakes as it is worn out. Lastly comes the indiarubber-like "frog," occupying the centre of the hoof, and being exactly analogous to the footpads of a dog or cat. To remove or lessen the frog, so as to throw all the weight on the crust, is like cutting away the foot-pads of the dog and making it walk on the tips of its claws.

The remarkable structure called the "external frog" is also meant for perpetually wearing away and renewal. It is not rubbed off like the horn of the crust, nor flaked off like that of the sole, but drops off in ragged flaps which need no touch of the farrier's knife, and will not produce thrush or any other ailment if suffered to remain until they fall of their own accord.

Now, if the hoof be protected from friction, as is the case when shoes are added, it is evident that the horn must be artificially removed. The use of the knife is therefore a necessity, as far as removing the crust goes, and even in Japan, where the shoes are tied and not nailed to the hoof, the crust has to be pared, just as those who do no hard manual work are obliged to pare their nails. It is also evident that as the hoof grows unequally it must be trimmed unequally, and more material must be removed where it grows fastest.

Secondly, as the hoof is elastic, it is evident that it ought not to be confined by a rigid and non-elastic shoe; and lastly, as in the untouched hoof the weight of the animal is thrown on the central "frog," toward which the various elastic structures converge, the shod hoof ought to allow of the same central bearing.

A very natural question is often asked by those who really wish to do their best for the horse, *i.e.* whether the frog could grow sufficiently to reach the ground when the shoe is on the foot. This it certainly can do, but if the shoe be a thick one, the frog will be obliged to increase to an abnormal depth, and therefore might wrench the sensitive tissues painfully if suddenly pressed

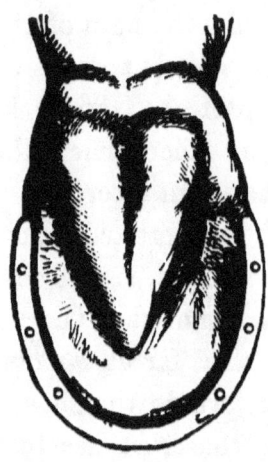

"CHARLIER" SHOE, MODIFIED BY FLEMING.

on one side. Our finger nails, if allowed to grow too long, are apt to produce the same effect.

There is one shoe, known as the "Charlier," which only covers the fore-part of the hoof, and which, being imbedded in the horn, does not raise the hoof off the ground, and so enables the frog to grow to its proper length. Some little care is needed in putting on the Charlier shoe, and it must be renewed at rather short intervals. But the ease and safety with which the horse so shod can tread, and the lightness of the weight attached to the hoof, are advantages which more than compensate for the trouble.

Within the last few years owners of horses have gradually come to understand the object of the frog, and have ordered their farriers to leave it untouched.

The opposition of nearly all farriers, and even of some veterinary surgeons, has been wonderfully aroused by the suggestion. In several places, I have found men who assert that "thrush" is produced by neglecting to cut the frog. The horn hangs from the uncut frog in ragged strips, and then, according to their ideas, the dirt works its way between them into the interior of the hoof, sets up inflammation, and causes thrush. Now I wonder how wild horses manage to trim their hoofs, and how many of them suffer from thrush.

During the controversy which has lately been aroused respecting the shoe and the hoof, it has been mentioned more than once that when a young horse has been ridden and driven without having his feet protected by shoes, he has gone admirably at first, but after he has travelled some miles his feet have given way, the hoofs being worn down to the quick, and the animal unable to move a step. Several persons who have tried the experiment and met with this result, have written to the effect that they have given the horse a fair trial without shoes, but that the hard artificial roads have been too much for him.

Such a result might have been expected. In every case when I had made inquiries it turned out that the horse had been taken from soft pasture land where he had passed all his previous life, and had been taken over the stony road without any preparation. Of course his hoofs gave way. But had he been kept for some time on hard, stony ground, such as is the natural condition for which the hoof is constructed, the horn would have become hard enough to perform its complex duties.

It is scarcely possible to find better advice than that which was given by Xenophon in his treatise on "Horsemanship," written somewhere about the time when the prophet Malachi lived.

No one was better qualified than Xenophon to give advice, and there is no one whose advice can demand more respect. As a general, the Wellington of his day; as a writer, the crystalline and artful simplicity of his style is curiously like that of our own Addison; as a hunter, and, indeed, in all kinds of sport, he was the acknowledged authority of his time, as is shown in his "Cyægeticus." With regard to the horse, the man who conducted that marvellous "Retreat of the Ten Thousand" over so long and difficult a track, was likely to understand the management of the horse's hoof. Here are some of his dicta.

"To prevent stable floors from being smooth, they should have stones similar to a horse's hoofs in size inserted in the ground, for such stable floors give firmness to the feet of horses that stand on them.

"The groom must also lead the horse out of the stable to the place where he is to comb him; and he should be tied away from the manger after his morning's feed, that he may come to his evening's meal with the greater appetite.

"The ground outside the stable may be put into excellent condition, and serve to strengthen the horse's feet, if a man lays down here and there four or five loads of round stones, each large enough to fill the two hands, and weighing about a pound, surrounding them with an iron rim, so that they may not be scattered. For, as the horse stands on these, he will be in much the same condition *as if he were to travel part of every day on a stony road.*

"A horse must also move his hoofs while he is being rubbed down, or when he is annoyed with flies, as much as when he is walking, and the stones which are thus spread about *strengthen the frogs of the feet.*"—" Horsemanship" ("Hipparchicus"), ch. iv. §§ 3—5. Watson's Translation.

The almost universal idea that the horse's hoof is all very well for its own country, but is unable to withstand the artificial roads of our country, is utterly absurd to those who know anything of the various soils habitually traversed by the wild horse. The very worst road in England is as a Turkey carpet to a new gravel walk when compared to the rocks, sands, morasses, sage-brush, and shingle, which the wild horse traverses with perfect ease. And I am sure that if we would only give the natural hoof a fair trial, it would be found equal to its work, whether for saddle or draught. It answers in Italy, where the roads are harder, steeper, and sharper, and more slippery than ours, and why it should not answer in England I cannot understand.

Here, for example, is an extract of a letter lately addressed by a resident in Naples to a friend in Bristol.

"Rome and Naples are both paved with lava, which, with the least frost becomes as slippery as our own roads in a frost. Most of the valuable horses were unshod on the hind feet, while some had no shoes on at all, and their hoofs were in capital condition, though the lava was as hard as granite." Only a few days before writing these lines, I was conversing with a friend who had lived for some time in Italy and gave a similar account, adding that even when the fore-feet were shod, the shoes were only small tips, or "half-moons," as they were called.

Considering the extreme cruelty with which the Italian treats his horses, it does seem wonderful that we, with our many societies for promoting the welfare of animals, and who pride ourselves on our superiority in this respect to other countries, have never given the horse a fair chance of using the natural feet as God made them. There must be many humane persons who are wealthy enough to try the experiment, and run the risk of failure; and energetic enough to anticipate and repulse those who will assuredly do all in their power to hinder its success.

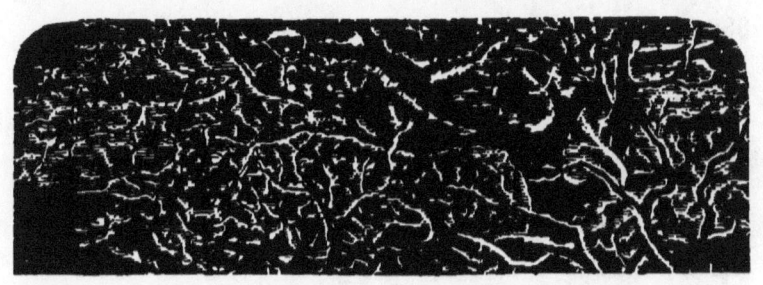

THE HORSE AND HIS STRUCTURE.

CHAPTER IV.

THE HEAD AND NECK.

HAST *thou* given the horse strength? Hast *thou* clothed his neck with thunder?

Who can be insensible to the magnificent utterances which, even in a language incapable of rendering the full beauty of the original tongue, throw all our modern poetry into the shade. Yet man, just as he neutralises by iron shoes the natural elasticity of the hoof, by means of various contrivances renders nugatory the exquisite mechanism of the bones, muscles, and ligaments from the neck to the shoulder.

I wonder whether any of my readers have ever thought about the structures which enable the horse to hold its head up without fatigue. *We* could not do it, and if we were placed on all fours, we should soon find our heads drooping from sheer fatigue.

If we place a hand on the back of our neck and bend the head forward, we shall feel a strong ligament. If the skin be removed, this ligament is seen to be cord-like, and not to present any very remarkable peculiarity of structure.

In the horse, however, it is developed into a most wonderful elastic mechanism. Lapping over the back of the neck, as shown in the illustration at A, it throws out a set of projections, each of which is fastened to one of the vertebræ of the neck in such a manner that, while it gives support to that particular vertebra, it works simultaneously with the others.

Thus, the animal can toss or shake its head, turn it round to its flanks, or depress it to its knees, the powerful and highly-elastic ligaments permitting all these movements, and by their own resilience restoring the head and neck to their normal position when the muscles are relaxed.

The weight of the head and neck is very considerable, and by their movements the balance of the body is materially aided, *e.g.*, in walking up a very steep hill, the horse when at liberty throws his head and neck well forward, so as to keep the weight as much as possible in *front* of the fore-feet. In descending the same hill, the horse holds his head and neck as far back as he can, so as to throw the weight *behind* the fore-feet.

Man, however, is pleased to fancy that this freedom of action looks mean and spiritless, and that a horse ought to hold his head up, no matter whether he is ascending

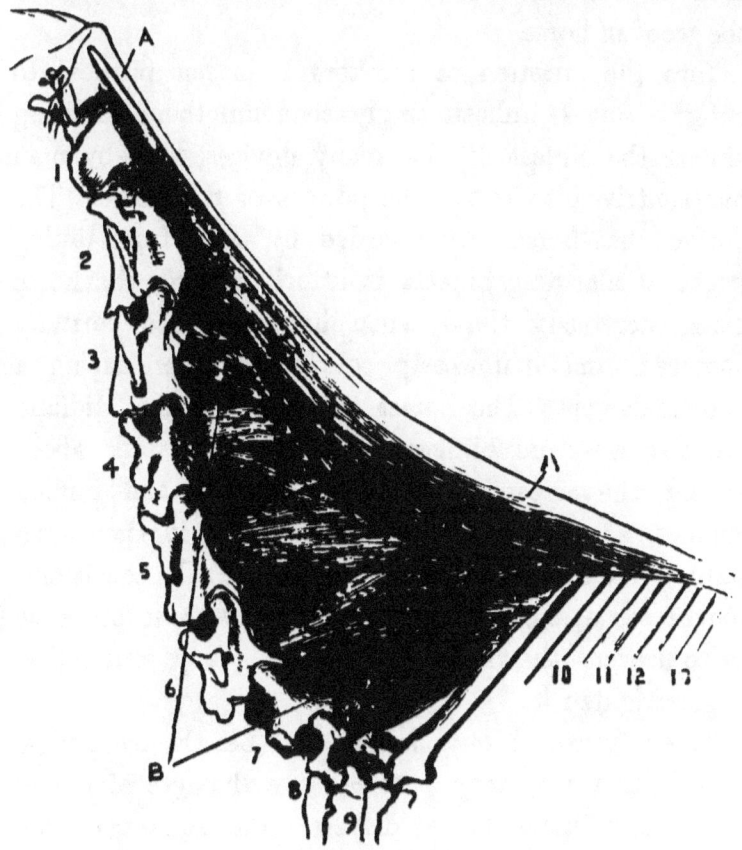

LIGAMENTS AND VERTEBRÆ OF THE HORSE'S HEAD.

or descending a hill, standing still, walking, trotting, or galloping. His model seems to be the wooden horse of the toy-shops, and the nearer approach that he can make to the stiff rigidity of the toy-horse, the better is he pleased. As if to increase the resemblance he even cuts the mane short—"hogs" it, as the expression is, so as to make it look like the strip of fur glued on the neck of the wooden horse.

Into the question of blinkers I do not purpose to enter. But I unhesitatingly condemn them as being among the silliest of the many devices whereby man has contrived to lessen the powers of the horse. The notion that horses are guarded by them from taking fright at alarming objects is utterly absurd, the horse being nervously timid when its senses are partially obscured, and dauntlessly courageous when facing a known danger. The horses employed on the Midland Railway wear no blinkers, and yet they walk about among the screaming whistles, snorting and puffing engines, as composedly as if they were in their own stables, not even requiring to be led. To be consistent, the horse's ears ought to be furnished with stoppers, so as to prevent the animal from hearing any sound that might frighten it.

The only excuse for blinkers that has the least sense in it is, that they may possibly save the eyes of horses from the whips of brutal drivers. But as no man who would flog a horse about the head ought to be intrusted with a horse, even this very lame defence breaks down.

Besides the reins, he attaches to the bit a leathern strip called a "bearing-rein"—I suppose because it is hard for the horse to bear—and fastens it to the saddle, so as to render the animal incapable of lowering its head beyond a certain point, according to the length of the rein. Not content with this, a still more severe instrument was invented, and is known by the name of the

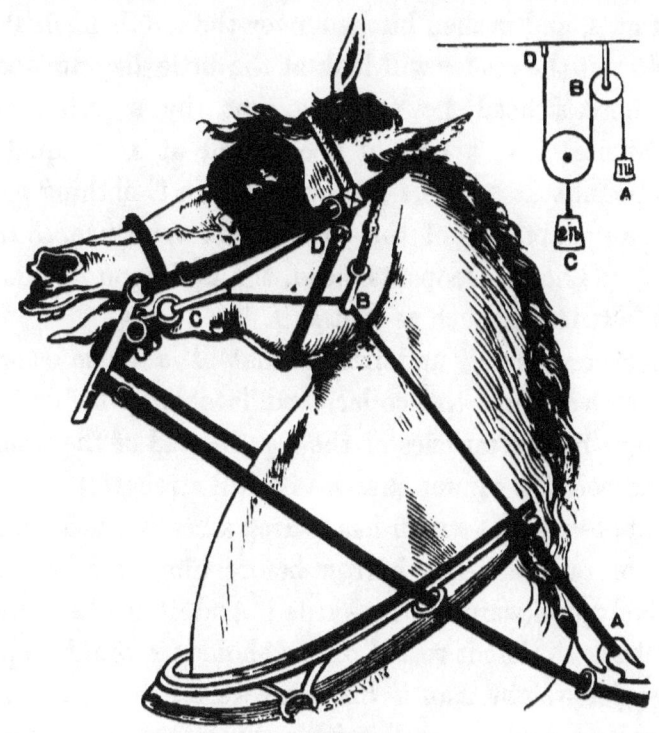

THE "GAG" BEARING-REIN.

"gag," or Bedouin, bearing rein. This apparatus is shown in our illustration.

In the ordinary bearing-rein, the strap is hitched upon the saddle-hook A, passes through the drop-ring at B, and is fastened to the bit at C. Thus, if the horse should droop its head, it is checked by the bearing-rein, the pull on the mouth at C being equal to that on the saddle at A.

But, the strap of the "gag" bearing-rein is not attached to the bit at all, but to the head-stall at D. Thence it passes through the swivel at C, then through the drop-ring at B, and is then hitched over the saddle-hook at A.

Now, if the reader will look at the little diagram above the horse's head, he will see that, by a well-known mechanical law, a pull of one pound at A is equal to two pounds at C. The gag bearing-rein is nothing more than an adaptation of this mechanical appliance, so that when the horse droops its head, the pull upon its mouth at C is twice as much as that at A.

Everyone must understand that if a horse cannot throw itself into the collar, and is obliged to draw a carriage by the muscles of the legs instead of the weight of the body, it cannot exercise its full strength.

Supposing that a man has to drag a heavy truck behind him, or push a heavy barrow before him, does he bend his body backwards or forwards ? And, if his head were tied back so that it rested on his shoulders, could he pull a heavier weight than if his head were free ? And, as to stumbling, could he walk with a surer foot upon uneven and stony ground if his head were dragged back so that he could not see the ground ?

I have already mentioned that cutting away the frog of the hoof was defended on the ground that it was a preventive of thrush, quitters, and other diseases. So there are thousands of human beings, possessed of average intellect, who really think that the bearing-rein is invaluable as a guard against stumbling and an absolute preventive of falling.

If the bearing-rein were fastened to the carriage-box, there might be some faint grounds for thinking that it could hold the horse up; but how a horse can be held up by tying his head to his own back, is ludicrously impossible. An amusing parallel is given by "Free-Lance" in one of his letters, wherein he asks whether a man can get into a clothes-basket, grasp the handles and lift himself off the ground.

Even if the rein were fastened to the carriage-box, it could not mend matters, for no rein is strong enough to sustain the weight of a horse. Many a bearing-rein has been broken by a falling horse, the instinctive flinging forwards of the head snapping the leather rein as if it were packthread. Even the hook has been dragged out of the saddle by the bearing-rein, and when we remember that the force was exerted upon the sensitive mouth of a horse, it is clear that cruelty is superadded to folly.

Another "reason" for the use of the gag bearing-rein is that it gives the horse such a noble appearance. People see the horse champing its bit, flinging foam-flakes right and left, tossing its head, rattling its harness, and assume that the horse is acting in the pride of its strength and fulness of spirit. Whereas it is suffering agonies of pain, and is trying to gain a momentary relief by these head-tossings and harness-rattlings.

Who ever saw a horse champ and foam at the mouth when at liberty? Or who ever saw a horse free in a field plant its fore and hind legs apart, curve its body backwards, and hold its head above its shoulders? Yet this is the attitude invariably assumed by "gagged" horses when standing in the streets. In fact, they are trying by pressure in front and behind, to contract the spine as much as possible, and so to relieve the intolerable pressure on the mouth.

Not long before these lines were written, I engaged a cab for the purpose of making a series of visits to a suburb of London.

I was struck with the fact that the driver never used his whip, and yet that the horse went quite freely, although the road had been recently "mended" by spreading flints and other stones of irregular sizes over it. On alighting, I told the driver that I had noticed that the whip had not been used, and the man replied that he had no whip, and never would use one.

The return journey being all up-hill, I determined to watch the man's mode of driving, and soon found that even the use of the reins was merely nominal, the man guiding the horse entirely by the voice.

After going some little distance the driver dismounted, and walked by the side of the horse. After a while, he turned the cab to the side of the road, and walked alone up the hill.

When he had gone fifty or sixty yards, he called to the horse, "Now, my lady, if you are quite rested, come on." She turned her head round, looked at him, and resumed her former position. She had *not* rested sufficiently. The man said, "All right," and continued to walk on. In a short time, the animal turned round of her own accord, and followed the man to the top of the hill.

Some weeks afterwards, I again had occasion to visit the same place. There was another driver and another cab. The horse behaved very strangely, jerking, jibbing, and occasionally stopping, though the road was in very good condition. The driver used his whip freely, jerked the reins, and bawled at the top of his voice, but the horse really seemed too feeble to take the carriage to its destination.

On alighting, I went up to the horse's head and found that there was a bearing-rein buckled as far back as possible. The horse was wet with perspiration, and fretting with nervous excitement. The driver said that he had put it on because the hills were so steep that he was afraid lest the horse should fall and break her knees on the loose stones. He then at my request took off the bearing-rein, and the demeanour of the animal was instantly changed.

To my astonishment, I then recognised the same grey mare whose behaviour had pleased me so much on the previous occasion, but so altered was she by the bearing-rein that I had not recognised her in the darkness.

The driver was not really a cruel man. He had done

what he thought was best for the horse, and was evidently interested when I explained the structure of the animal.

When the time for returning drew near I recognised the footsteps of the grey mare as she came trotting freely along. The driver had not replaced the bearing-rein, and without a touch of the whip the horse trotted off with a freedom of motion wonderfully contrasting with the fretful jerks and jibbings.

Happily, the campaign against the bearing-rein, so energetically conducted by Mr. E. F. Flower, is doing its work, and people are beginning to realise the fact that the horse can do more with a free head than a cramped one. Perphaps they may make one short advance, and after freeing his mouth from the bearing-rein, and his eyes from the blinkers, will release his feet from the iron shoes.

THE END.

www.ingramcontent.com/pod-product-compliance
Lightning Source LLC
Chambersburg PA
CBHW031847220426
43663CB00006B/528